POLISHING THE PE͜ͅ

Polishing the Petoskey Stone

selected
poems

Luci Shaw

REGENT COLLEGE PUBLISHING
VANCOUVER, BRITISH COLUMBIA

First published 1990 by Harold Shaw Publishers

This edition published 2003 by Regent College Publishing
5800 University Boulevard, Vancouver, BC V6T 2E4 Canada
www.regentpublishing.com

Views expressed in works published by Regent College Publishing are those
of the authors and do not necessarily represent the views or opinions of
Regent College.

Grateful acknowledgement is made to the editors of the following publica-
tions in which these poems were first printed: *The Reformed Journal* for
"Caged bird," "Wild bees' nest," "Polishing the Petoskey Stone," "Slide
Photography: Climbing the Mount of Olives," "The amphibian,"
"Omnipotence," "Subliminal messages," "Raspberries," "Travelling
Montana"; *Time of Singing* for "Designer"; *Today's Christian Woman* for
"Quiltmaker"; *U* for "Son and Mother"; *Christianity & Literature* for
"Airborne over Idaho," "Paraousia: The ghosts in the closet," "Road to
Oregon coast"; *Image* for "Sudden Valley Road"; Zondervan Publishing
Corporation for "Fair, clear & terrible," "How to paint a promise in
January," "Questions: 1985" in *God in the Dark*, © 1989 by Luci Shaw.

The following sections first appeared in previous volumes of poetry by Luci
Shaw and were published by Harold Shaw Publishers:

Listen to the Green, © 1971
The Secret Trees, © 1976
The Sighting, © 1981
Postcard from the Shore, © 1985

National Library of Canada Cataloguing in Publication Data

Shaw, Luci
  Polishing the Petoskey stone / Luci Shaw.

  Poems.
  ISBN 1-55361-077-6 (Canada)
  ISBN 1-57383-243-X (United States)

  I. Title.

PS3569.H384P58 2003   811'.54   C2003-910190-8

for Carolyn

Contents

LISTEN TO THE GREEN

THE SECRET TREES

THE SIGHTING

POSTCARD FROM THE SHORE

Foreword

The young nun who wanted to learn to pray was sent by Teresa of Avila to the pots and pans in the monastery kitchen. William Blake saw eternity in a grain of sand. Julian of Norwich saw all the operations of God in a hazel nut. Sunrays splashed on a pewter plate and Jacob Boehme beheld the glory. Such are the raw materials of sanctity. Not ecstasy. Not visions. Not genius.

We know this, or at least we know about it, from our mentors. But we require more than instruction, we need *demonstration;* we want to see how it works. Luci Shaw, "a poet sorting socks," shows us how it works. Her poems are a generous workshop in the operations of sanctity. I have been carrying around one thin book after another of her poems for years, reading them, letting them be read to me—watching, listening. I use them for environmental protection: they filter noise out of the air so I hear quiet sounds breathing creation into being each morning; they scrub crude-oil grime from the landscape so I see contours in faces and fields and furniture that are containers for grace. The sights and sounds were there all the time, but habit and cliché and hurry obscured them. The poems whisper "holy, holy, holy" *here, now.* Before I know it and without moving an inch, I have stepped into sacred space, sacred time. I am participant in just a little more reality (sometimes a lot more) than before.

Luci Shaw, for me, has been one of those poets admired by Wallace Stevens who "most urgently search the world for the sanctions of life, for that which makes life so prodigiously worth living . . . (and) find their solutions in a duck in a pond or in the wind on a winter night." I like her energy ("urgently search"); I like the sacramental undertow ("sanctions of life"); I like the affirmations wrestled out of darkness ("prodigiously worth living").

Tired stories, dustcovered names, and habit-dulled sights take a swim in her imagination and emerge on the shoreline of her poems glistening: Jonah arrives "damp but undigested"; a tree in a storm points "the way the wind/went"; earthworms "drilling the soil,/digesting it" get included in divinity; the embryonic Jesus is "infinity walled in a womb"; the shy and complex world of adolescent sexuality is comprehended in an apple hefted and halved; on a spring walk through the woods "all trilliums unfold/white flames above their trinities/of leaves"; and not infrequently, while sitting in worship, with her I see "shining arcs of praise/held at their lower ends/by the old hymns."

And more. Much more. She does this so well—takes place and weather, worship and adoration, death and doubt, family and faith and locates them with spiritual honesty and verbal precision in the life of pilgrimage. Longtime readers of these poems will renew old acquaintances and pick up a sheaf of new friends besides. New readers will welcome her gifts of word-crafted icons by which we behold the Glory, see the Holy.

Eugene H. Peterson

Introduction

It has been said that faith is "a certain widening of the imagination." When Mary asked the Angel, "How shall these things be?" she was asking God to widen her imagination.

All my life I have been requesting the same thing—a baptized imagination that has a wide enough faith to see the numinous in the ordinary. Without discarding reason, or analysis, I seek from my Muse, the Holy Spirit, images that will open up reality and pull me in to its center.

This is the benison of the sacramental view of life—that all of existence falls under the provenance of God. The Logos not only spoke the universe into being; he still embraces it, defining and re-defining it, assigning it meaning and value at every level. As C.S. Lewis put it: "I believe in Christianity as I believe the sun has risen, not only because I see it but because by it I see everything else."

I hold in my hand three smooth stones—Petoskey stones. There is a story to them—really a story within a story.

Several years ago my friend Carolyn and I chartered a 28-foot sailboat for a week of Great Lakes sailing. She was newly divorced; I was newly widowed. Both of us were questioning our ability to navigate the waters which stretched all around us to the horizon, both geographically and spiritually.

Sailing out of Green Bay, Wisconsin, we crossed the featureless 65-mile width of Lake Michigan, out of sight of land for hours at a time, depending on compass, charts, depth sounder, and the angle of the wind to determine our position and our heading and find our destination on the opposite shore.

Sailing north along the eastern rim of the lake Carolyn remarked, "We ought to swim ashore and look for Petoskey stones." Anchoring, and moving from the macro to the microcosm, we swam the quarter mile toward the land—no sandy beach, but a boulder-strewn margin, sharp under our bare feet. As we hopped from rock to rock I asked Carolyn, "So, what *is* a Petoskey stone?"

This is what I learned: It's all that is left of a soft, six-sided coral (*Hexagonaria*) that grew in colonies across what is now Upper Michigan when it was covered, 350 million years ago, by a tropical sea.

Petoskey stones are found nowhere else in all the world. The grey fossil chunks, now broken and rounded into pebbles by the waves, still show the faint markings of the hexagonal structures into which the coral stalks crowded when they were growing. These mineral families, in an excess of pre-human efficiency, found the pattern which has the greatest structural strength and wastes the least space— an arrangement much like the cells in a honeycomb. The coral was first identified in the small Michigan town of Petoskey, hence its name.

At first glance Petoskey stones are not particularly attractive, almost indistinguishable from other dull, grey, shore stones. But if you have sharp eyes you can pick them out. Carolyn showed me a trick. "Spit on them, or dunk them in the water and rub them. Then you'll see the pattern." We found half a dozen fine specimens, and our enthusiasm escalated.

Later, with the boat berthed in Petoskey, we discovered shining samples of the stones in every gift shop—uniformly beautiful after having been polished in gem tumblers, their fine, lace-like patterns, grey on grey, precisely defined.

Carolyn told me that it is possible to polish the stone even without a mechanical tumbler. Later that summer when I drove from Wheaton to Wichita, where I was to work on a new book at Friends University, I took a lovely oval stone in the car with me and rubbed it as I drove for almost a thousand miles—on the velour seat covers, on my jeans, on my wool sweater. As the stone gradually revealed itself to me, I wrote in my mind the poem that is on p. 8.

I rarely sit down to write an explicitly "Christian" poem. But I find that as I allow the created universe and the ingrained Scripture to illuminate me, what I deeply believe pushes up through the fabric of words. The poem had been completed for nearly a year before I began to recognize new levels of its meaning.

Near the end of that year, on another sailing trip in the same area, Carolyn and I spent a couple of mornings at anchor, on deck, polishing rough Petoskey stones with emery paper and emery powder from a gift shop in town. You have to work the stones wet, rubbing away at the rough greyness, rinsing in clear water, then rubbing, rinsing, until you achieve a gloss. As the pattern became increasingly clear—six-sided growths outlined with fine spines like eyelashes—some correspondences rose to the surface of my mind:

I saw a living stone, a dying and burial in a sea of baptism, the sleep of death, an awakening of this creature to new life and "consciousness." I saw burden-bearing, and someone else's "polishing" as the mode of personal awakening and revelation. I saw a baby, cradled, rocked, held tenderly until it opened its eyes. I saw the deliberateness of God's emery powder working over each roughness *by hand* until the sheen caught and held the light—a process different from the indiscriminate action of waves (or gem tumblers) which reduce all stones to a kind of uniformity.

The revealed pattern in a Petoskey stone looks like eyes. The surface is semi-transparent; that is, when the stone is burnished smooth as glass you can see deep into it, as if to its "soul," and feel that it is looking back at you, as each of us looks back at God with our inner eyes when we sense he is focussing in on us. Thus, we can engage in a dialogue of searching glances.

I feel like a Petoskey stone, once grey and dull, but now achieving a gloss that shows it for what it is. And I know who is doing the polishing.

Polishing the Petoskey Stone

1986-1990

The amphibian

Warm
after a while on a rock,
drunk with sky, her green silk
shrivels with wind. With a wet,
singular sound, then, she creases
the silver film, turns fluid,
her webbed toes accomplishing
the dark dive to water bottom and
the long soak, until her lungs,
spun for air, urge her up
for breath.

She moves
in two worlds, caught between
upper and under, never home.
Restless: skin withering for wet,
and the nether ooze,
or nostrils aching to fill
with free air her bubble lungs,
heart thumping, tympanum
throat pulsing to flood
the darkening sky with loud
frog song.

Conch

Its open mouth corresponds
to your own hunger to hear.
Rough as the bleat
of gulls, its edges
rasp your cheek, cold as salt;
the surge of sound floods
into your own convoluted
shell of an ear
through tympanum, stapes, cochlea.

You lean into the roar—a tide
of air and water trapped
at the pink, helical heart—
an ocean tumbled over
and over. Breath still moves
on the face of the deep;
you ache to its
tempest at your cheekbone.
And the inside tremor—the thunder,
the wave that breaks over
more than your bare feet.

Listen deep until it drowns you.
Know the whole world
a shell, and you the grit
caught in it, being pearled over.

Beachcomber

satin black, three stones
lie warm in my palm—a handful
of shore in my room

Seasleeping: Cape Cod

Lying in bed with
the evening window
open to the bay
I feel his kinship
with the sea: he's like
the waves that reach
for me as they
accomplish a kind of
breathing—again and
again a push and a pull
to the limits.
        As each
crest and the next
breaks and retreats from
a foreplay of foam, our
inlet is replenished
with a salt wash,
cloudy with sand,
warmed by its brief
excursion,
        leaving me
smooth as a dune, polished,
winking in subdued light,
lapped by a husband
whose every draft of air
swells, pauses, retreats
with a silver sigh.
        Like
a sandbar I shift
under the weight of an
ocean until the tide
fills our whole bay.
It is then that the wind
flattens, and a skin of
silence settles
like a sheet
over our midnight sleep.

Worldview

*"Color pattern on underside of tail
can be read like a fingerprint. Reaches
50' long."*
　　　—from a New England postcard picturing
　　　　a humpback whale

Like a flag in a gust
she unfurls. The present
tense, she powers up
from the pull of gravity.
Breaching in gargantuan play,
fluting her flukes'
unduplicated under-sides,
she leaps—slow motion—
shedding a shroud of foam.
Ropes of watered pearls slide
from her shoulders. When she blows,
it is a triumph of spume
inviting rainbows.

Standing on her single, muscular
foot as if the sea were solid—
a pedestal for sight-
seeing—she views the world.
Lifting that great weight
like an offering
she swims the ocean of air, flouts
the horizon's rule. In one
steel fling she sounds the sky,
flashes, falls, sinks, begins
again the search for the deep place
of her final and inevitable sleep.

Polishing the Petoskey Stone

Petoskey Stone (Hexagonaria)—a petrified colony coral 350 million years old, found on beaches in Michigan

My friend says, "Spit on it, and rub
the surface. See the pattern?"
In its hammock of lines I lift the pebble
the color of a rain cloud, cradle it
a thousand miles. Holding

the steering wheel in one hand, the grey
oval curved to my other palm, we move,
a ripple across the map to Kansas, while
I rub its softness in ellipses
against a rough shore of denim and wool.

The second day it starts
to shine like glycerin soap. As I buff it
smooth, the print rises to the surface—
the silk stone honeycombed with
eyes opening from a long sleep

between lashes of fine spines. Born
eons ago in a warm sea over
Michigan, buried in a long, restless
dream, now the old coral wakes
to the waves of cloth.

Travelling Montana
for Karen Cooper

Back then, the spreading
glitter of it (you
were driving) pressed the sights
onto the bound pages waiting, bland
on my lap; the barbwire—frost-whiskered
for miles, a running accompaniment
to the road, the gelid slurry of gravel
on the cold shoulder, the sliding by
of the river under a Holy Ghostly
cloak of steam were written there
at 60 mph and 20 below, plucked out of
a moving landscape, fastened
to a lined sheet by
the pointed pin of ink.

Here it is still, dog-eared
in my old journal. As I copy it
into a letter to you, as your eyes pull
the words through thin air
Image will turn *thing* again
and teach us each from its veracity.
Far as we are now—Vancouver to
Chicago—December to June—
the syllables will doubly sketch
the cold light of that morning
until our separate skins again
turn white as frostbite.

It is a stronger icon now
than I noticed at the time, simplified,
minus the adjuncts.
The shapes will flicker in your mind
differently than for me. My scene
has hardened; vapor in the navels of

the valleys has been bleached like
woodpulp—flat as paper. How is it
for you? Driving your mind back
under the Big Sky, can you reinvent it
and chart your own route east?

Aviation symptoms

I know someone from Wyoming
with all the aviation symptoms—
hyperventilation, levity, budding
scapular extensions, cloud
nine tendencies beginning with
euphoria and anorexia (sure signs
of early weightlessness).

Addicted to air he feels the city
heavy. Earth-bound, he knows he must
rise on the updraughts between all those
perpendiculars like a bit
of confetti, unpredictable as a
virus. The pigeons will despise him;
he cannot shit white or find his place
on the sunny side of a cathedral roof.
The comedy of his disease as his
slightness must be shifted
from foot to foot! The drag of
hot-core down-below magma still
prevails over the faint magnetism
of moons, cold as vanilla ice
spilled in a city gutter.

Gravity cannot hold him. He's phobic—
I acknowledge it. And possibly
evaporation (his edges are blurring
already, frayed by space) is catching
and my own anxiety for him will
float, erratic as litter in any windy
city, and infect all of us
with an incurable lightness.

The trouble with trouble

No doubt about it, pain
puts to the test
the rubric of anatomy,
scours the arteries,
puffs the lungs, accelerates
the heart, pleats the nerves
tight to their lowest threshold,
even teaches the brain
to be a kind of muscle.

Here comes a pang. Watch—
even the rectangles
of light narrow to
razors, the shadows
on the wall darken like
bruises. Every color looks
sanguine, but without hope.

Deciding, I plant myself
steady as an anvil, study
how receiving a blow
cancels the action:
what changes me is what
I change. In this crucible
things melt or harden.
Irreversibly; either
I am gold, bleeding
a yellow mirror, or a damp
clay set out for firing.

The heat is on; blows number
the minutes; anguish
begins over again
to bring me to my senses.

Sudden Valley Road

DEATH HERE
AUTO ACCIDENT
FRIDAY, APRIL 1

It stares at me as if
I did it—the cardboard sign, fog-warped,
stained by the steady grief of rain.
Nailed to a phone pole beside the
rising slick of the road, the black letters signal
something too huge to say. Like a white
flag that stands for a whole army
in surrender, its skewed rectangle shrinks
the truth, forces me to fill the details in
as I bank on the steep curve,
tires skidding. I feel it
all the way down the other side—
how it would be to lie there,
spilled along the gravel, body
ragged as the maple leaves bleeding
around the bend, eyes milky
under the shroud that fogs the mountain.

Somehow the notice is fastened
to a death that still
shudders around the curving world
whose naked placard, tacked to a post,
affronts all of us fools, through the drizzle
of years, as though we did it.

Questions: 1985

Beside me, under the sheet, his shape
is blurred, his breath irregular, racing
or slowing to the stress/release
of dreams. One lung—a wing of air—
has been already clipped. The scans
show the dark shadows on his bones.

His house of cells—blue-printed
by heredity, assembled season
by season, (the grayed wood
shrinking a little at the joins
under the wash of time and storm)
—will it collapse like a barn
settling into its field?
His spirit—iridescent as a pigeon
—will it escape before mine
through a break in the roof,
homing, homing through the sky?

Parousia: The ghosts in the closet

A
small
space full of
shapes on hangers,
deserted, waiting there
thin, flat as sardines in a
can. What if he came back, and
life breathed into them, hard, like
balloons; if at his touch on the switch
yellow light crowded the corners,
the door burst open and, with
a jostle of cloth, they
all surged out and
left me with
nothing to
wear at
all
?

Subliminal messages
for Harold Fickett

The telephone is silent; God doesn't return
   my calls to the office.
We're supposed to be married, but I think
   he's left me, gone
on a long trip to the Antarctic—somewhere
   cold.
The pleading letters I write him pile up,
   unsent, on the hall table;
I have no forwarding address for declarations
   of desire, invitations
to come back to me, flowers, a new book,
   a birthday present in December.
Living in the dumbness of a dead phone, an
   empty mailbox,
always, when I get home from work, the house
   is dark, the dog bored,
the plants browning, the sink piled with
   my own dirty dishes.

But yesterday the sun came out for half
   an hour, whitening the curtains
from outside. Maybe it was a message,
   subliminal,
like the Two Part Inventions on the car
   radio
with Bach's questions and answers—two voices
   in conversation,
or the way the wind strokes the roof
   at night
or the rain tracks down the window glass,
   intimate as tears.

Omnipotence

He asks of us a big
faith—the moving
of mountains. It fits—
he was the one who
made a Big Bang,
spins a galaxy like
a child's top,
cradles our world
—a marble in his palm.
But can he pop
a jammed hood? Or deflate
an aneurism? Is he
deft enough to splint
a broken finger, split
an apple between us,
or flick a loose lash
from my eye?

He's big alright—his face
could brood
from Mount Rushmore.
But I ache for
a God my size to bring me
hot chocolate, brush
my hair, slip
between my sheets,
read to me in bed.
For a lover like that
I'd move a mountain
one stone at a time.

Airborne over Idaho

Airborne, over Idaho,
I am uncertain where you are.
So human, caught in your
bone box like me, through
the cracks of sense
you perceived the world
you knew already; touch
taught you the surfaces
of things; movement
filled your ears like
leaves in a wind. The breeze
compassed your nose with a spill
of clues. On your tongue,
it all tasted salt—tears,
Dead Seas, leaking bloods.
Sight—the inner images,
the view from the brow
of the cliff, congealed in your
memory, as it does in mine.

Yes. It is your humanity
I long to suck at all day long,
like a lozenge under the tongue.
But I am the Twin, truly,
blinking to focus your
unduplicated face in my mind's
eye, longing for the lost look
and feel of you, the jut of nose,
angles of eyes and mouth,
sheath of skin, burning voice
creating, recreating with a word.

And without palpability,
what? I am alone in this mystery,
an interior place. The stream of wind
passes the plexiglass unfelt.
Either I have a blank for a God

or a flawed faith that cannot
fill the detail in.
At this height I am in space
about myself as well, remote,
waiting for final touchdown,
aching for your arm to go
around my shoulders when I
meet you at the gate.

In the bedroom: dreaming back

Blowing, our morning curtains'
polished cloth shines with flowers
more permanent, less real, than blooms
of tufted cotton leaping in a field
of air. The bedframe's wood echoes
the gong of wind. The white rug seems
to move, restless as early sun
on the backs of sheep, slow as my own
solitary waking. The door's brass knob,
the window glass, with his
smudged prints still showing, smelt
in their mineral memory, gel in the
early chill. On the dresser, paper
in the silver frame lives back its layers
—photo, to dried pulp, to the cells
of a forest that was standing
long before we came together, and after
he left.

July 7, 1988

Raspberries

Robins and chickadees, quick as
scissors, are there first,
sighting along the hairy stems,
slanting under leaves, darting
between thorns to the hearts,
pendant as jewels.

The birds think the berries
theirs, and us the shameless thieves.
Our human neighbor, too, is adversarial.
Always the primitive growth threatens
to prickle into his acre,
and last May he fired our canes
(while we were gone) not knowing
you can't get rid of raspberries
that way—up from their small holocaust
they grew back twice as thick.

Today, undaunted by the scowl
from next door, I hunker down, squinting,
against the sun, lifting aside
the leaves, plunging my whole arm
to a bush's heart, my skin crossed
with beaded wires of blood,
my palms bright with a sweet serum.
Thinking thorns, and blood, and fruit,
I take into my fingers, bit by bit,
the sum of summer.

If you care for me

speak to me without words
in a spiral of starlings
thrown into a bank of wind, scarves
of an invisible dancer
making the sky a stage

Make a negligent gesture like
the drop of a chestnut at my feet
the glossy nucula bounding out of its spiky casing
rolling to me, a gift round
and brown as a chocolate cream

Caress me with a curtain of dew
on my moonlit skylight, or boulders
shining under their clear skin
of rain. In the rock garden
a crimson cosmos articulates
its bright, small world. Speak
to my eyes in syllables of light
and color, if you care for me

Remind me about space as
I watch the finches
peck at the wind in the balsams. The doe
cleaves the air current over
the ribbon of creek. The great
blue heron elbows its way up
through gaps wild with branches
and you are opening
for me, too, a new passage
between the trees

By the way you breathe dead leaves
into a small whirlwind of fire
show me, if you care for me, how you can
lift me from the dust,
light me like tinder

Bringing back the mail

Near the cabin green air
rims every view and water
slides away in the creek bed
below my line of vision.
I carry four letters
back from the box
balanced in perilous air so thin
it gives way before my face.

Air's quicker than water, eddying
around the corner of the garage,
a vehicle for loose yellow leaves
but also shaped by smoke
as it climbs hot from the chimney.
And lighter. Water's held by its own
weight until it evaporates. Air
is fickle; I cannot hold it in my fist.

The brook drags enough to be noisy,
its amber knuckles rolling pebbles
in a mutter of sound that surrounds me
at the back door. Air at its fiercest
only sighs through intricacies of leaves
or moans in the green bottle that I blow
sometimes, across its small
mouth. The tone rises; unlike the brook

its music isn't so drained off
by gravity. Light is even lighter,
flaking and glittering from
the foiled water, a levity so subtle
that I barely notice when
it sheets away, up, over the hill,
a tide beginning its liquid ebb as
I read the fourth letter.

Road to the Oregon coast
A journal for Margaret

The road sign reads "Congestion."
Among the conifers I glimpse three
retiring cottages and a gas pump.

Ragged windows begin to tear
in the clouds. The blue at the horizon
is an innocence clean as forget-me-nots
through a telephoto lens; at apogee
the color burns enough to paint
the inside of anyone's skull.

The oatfield glitters dew-jade in
sun sudden as a flash bulb. The banks
drift daisies and white clover.

Though the signs say "Thickly Settled,"
and promise "Deer, Elk, next 10 M."
for a while I see nothing but spruce
crowded with indigo jays.

How do I decide what to
spend film on when I don't
know what's ahead? This moment's
now (river, deer drinking in
her reflected image) will not be
repeated, calls me to pay attention.
My camera buys the present a click
at a time, like a coin in a slot.

Beside me on the seat is a
hydrangea head; its fleshy petals
shift between rose, mauve,
stone blue—azure beads at each center.
I can't help it. I pull
to the gravel shoulder and take
its portrait an hour after I took

a parting shot at my hosts on their
front steps—a Portland Gothic—David
wild and shy in cerulean
socks, Jo with one eye shut, Chip
gazing narrowly, a scholar in bare feet.
"Look solemn," I said, as I focused,
because they did.

When the placards begin to repeat
themselves—"Ocean Beaches"—I begin
to think salt and gulls and sea oats.
A crest of dunes
and scattered cottages
occludes the horizon. Camera at the ready
I can still only intuit waves and
hard, flat sands,
but the air is charged with the smell
of brine, the pull of the tide.

These are the true signs;
we know when we see them.

The fixity of rocks

Swimming out to the gem rock
(polished by ice and set solitary,
its winter bondage melted
three weeks back)
the cold uncertainties of water
surround me, shrivel my gut,
shrink my leg muscles to a numbness
that feels almost warm.
The drag of the dark lake
seems more than gravity.

Halfway there, a sharp cramp. I know
what to do—extend the calf muscle to
its length. Relax
in a forced float.
Wait it out.

OK, now. Sidestroke. The change
of motion faces me to the sun;
I splutter as waves wash
into my mouth

until I see, solid under me
through the water's blue green,
a sub-marine shape.
My ankle bone scrapes it, it is
so real. Algae slimes the slope.
I scrabble for a clean hold until
the upper rock feels dry, hot,
under the heel of my hand, flat,
fixed. Stretching
on the mineral plateau, like
a fish on a plate, slows
my breathing. My heart settles,
my skin warms with waiting.
A slow strength flows back
for the swim back.

Winter chestnut: Five haiku
for Madeleine

Behind me—a thud
on the sidewalk, padded with
leaves like open hands.

I turn. It is like
a key. The jade womb unlocks
birthing you at my feet.

New as a baby
you hold the heavy secrets
of growing, dying.

Now fingered and shrunk,
your Fall gloss faded, you look
as spent as I feel,

But still you ride my
raincoat pocket—Christ's coal for
my five cold fingers.

Flower head

"We have the mind of Christ."

Perched on the high end of its
spinal stalk the brain blooms
like a pink cabbage rose

Peel back the blunt bone like a bud—
it will be meaty to touch, the
corolla folding in, folding in to echo
within the sepal skull
a blink of light, logarithms, a view
of ships in harbor, a word just now
rescued by memory, clipped arbor vitae,
how it smells—spiced

Here God lives, burrowing among
the petals, cross-
pollinating. Here is Christ's mind
juiced, joined, fleshed, celled.
Here is the clash,
the roil, an invasion, not gentle
as dew; the rose is unfurled
violently until the scent explodes
and detonates in the air

And oh, it trembles—
thousands of seeds ripen in it as
it reels in the wind

How to paint a promise in January
for Lauren

Here in my winter breakfast room,
the colors of rainbows are
reduced to eight solid lozenges in a
white metal tray. A child's brush
muddies them to gray in a
glass of water. Even the light breaks down
as it pushes through the rain-streaked
windows and polishes the wooden table
imperfectly.

                Green leaves always turn
brown. Summer died into the dark days
a long time ago; it is hard even to
remember what it was like, stalled
as I am in this narrow slot of time
and daylight.

                Until I look down again
and see, puddling along the paper,
under a painted orange sun
primitive as the first spoked wheel,
the ribbon of color flowing out of
my grand-daughter's memory—a new
rainbow, arc-ing wet over strokes of grass
green enough to be true.

Caged bird

whose eye,
bead-bright,
no longer
scans the sky—
whose sleek
shape, carved
for flight,
is shrouded
by a pall
of wire—
whose beak
sorts millet,
never finds
the sun-filled
film and fire
of insect wings,
nor worm's wry
juice: his
trinities
of claws grip
steel,
ache for real
bark, and the
fling of winds
and trees.

Birdness
blunted
by thin chrome,
he learns
all summer long
to sing
newly, to poem
his stunted
narrowness
in one long,

strong,
ascending,
airborne, sun-
colored wing
of song.

Wild oats

I

You narrow heads all bend the same
way, away from the wind. You

little bone beaks needle
the horizon.

Profligacy sucked you thin, drained
the frail green from your straws.

Still, you sow your itch prodigally
into the dry view, insatiable.

Transparent as lace, your frailty
beguiles us with a fine foolsgold.

But your promise falls flat; yields
no edible harvest; nourishes no one.

II

Like an insect a wild oat seed
drills the sod.

Only a long leg like a cricket
sticks up to mark the place.

Quiltmaker

*"I make them warm to keep my family from
freezing; I make them beautiful to keep my heart
from breaking."*
                              —prairie woman, 1870

To keep a husband and five children warm,
she quilts them covers thick as drifts against
the door. Through every fleshy square white threads
needle their almost invisible tracks; her hours
count each small suture that holds together
the raw-cut, uncolored edges of her life.

She pieces each one beautiful, and summer bright
to thaw her frozen soul. Under her fingers
the scraps grow to green birds and purple
improbable leaves; deeper than calico, her mid-winter
mind bursts into flowers. She watches them unfold
between the double stars, the wedding rings.

Presents

What's so good as getting?
The anticipation, snow
in the air, people with lists,
voices that drop when you
enter the room, the pine-wood
fire smell and the smell of pine
needles from the trimmed tree
by the window—it all narrows down
to the heft of the package in the
hands, the wondering, the unwrapping
(Careful—the paper's too pretty
to tear), the oh, the ah. What's
so good as getting

if not giving?
The covert questions, the catalogs
with corners turned back, the love
that overlooks cost, the hiding place
in the hamper, the card whose
colored words can't say it all,
the glee of linking want/wish
with have/hold, the handing over,
fingers brushing, the thing
revealed, the spark as the eyes
meet, and the hug. What's
as good as giving?

The little cat

Black—her head
half-shows in
my white doorway
not moving

We stare
at each other
both so solemn
I blink

and she's
gone, as though
I banished her
with my eyelids

Lullaby for Jack

I'll polish your face with the sun at noon.
I'll feed you the moon on a silver spoon.
With stars from a midnight sky wide-flung,
I'll sprinkle your hair, tickle your tongue.

Wild bees' nest

Elegant and spare as Samson's riddle
   you garnish a lion flank,
the angle of an eave, a hole abandoned
   by rabbits. Your habitat of wings
knits its steady, electronic hum.
   Your hexagons hark back to
old architectures of crystal.
   Fitting tongue-and-groove, you are
functional as paper; your walls
   push against the weight of air,
publish a corrugated strength.
   Like vases, your cylinders fill with
larvae, honey—a comb fit for a queen.

Designer

How elegant the egg—
though breakable, benign
and self-complete.
Its fluid shape how fine,
sans superfluity, and with
what firm economy of line.
How easily it fits the palm,
catches and holds a shine,
enters the eye, and rests
its case for the divine—
for elemental,
unimproved design!

Parabolas

1

After a full tree has grown from my mustard seed
the birds will build nests in the branches
and you will hear their singing all day long.
Listen—can you hear them singing all day long?

2

Happy is my heart soil when it is soft and dark
welcoming spring and a scatter of seeds. Look,
now, Sower: I have grown a skirt of new green,
and wind shadows the silk. Watch—soon
the fingers of air will tug at my harvest tassels.

3

After I have sold my house, cows, my ten
acres, truck, cashed in my savings bonds
and taken a shopping cart of cash to the
pearl dealer's, how radiantly will the one
great pearl glisten in my wife's naked bosom!

4

It is only after pushing for hours against
the dark wind, after the bite of brambles,
the rescue in the rain, with the found lamb's
heart still thundering against my own, that my
shepherd soul is restored, that I myself can rest
in the fold, and feed my flock in home pastures.

5

The lazy lilies, blooming over there,
wasting their sweetness on the summer air
lend me a metaphor and certify that I
may waste my wanton praising on the sky.

(The words parable *and* parabola *have a common source
in the Greek* paraballein—*to set or throw down beside,
implying juxtaposition, comparison, parallelism.)*

City set on a hill

The four wide bowls of oil,
cap a rectangle of columns
in the dark house of God. The discarded
linen clothes of priests
have been pulled into wicks,
thousands of them, like stalks
growing in each bowl, floating,
drawing up the oil of olives
into flowerbeds of light so that
through shadowed Jerusalem petals
wave from the flamelight
until the rising sun outshines them.

At midnight they show us how to be
wicks to bloom the oil to light,
then to become what we face
as light fills the early bowl of sky,
to be what moon is to sun—
mirror, solar cell, chloroplast,
soaking up the bright resin until
our own faces shine like noon.

Fair, clear, & terrible

The silver syllable of the new moon speaks the sky.
The trumpet of noon sun articulates zeniths, both past
and to come. Praise! for the plush fields, but also for
wry rocks and the dry, dying brass of deserts. *Gloria,*
   Domine,
for minds ignited with images, for the flames that leap from
God's tongue to scorch our pages with his true words.
   Exultate!

All sensate beings—Sing, from the throat! With the sting
of stigmata, of holy wounds, sharpening the sound,
   weaving
the waft of pleasurable air with the colored warp of pain.
Sing! For he comes, his nimbus a rainbow, fair as sun,
clear as moon, terrible as an army with banners glittering.
   Jubilate!

Like lightning he fires the fine hairs on our heads
till they gleam and flare—gold threads, silver. He polishes
the balls and sockets of our bones unto leaping and
   shivering.
Our loins burn. Our mouths are bells. Our hearts pulse
with holy desire, are transfixed by an invading grace, rise
to run, spirited, wearing the weight of glory given.
   Laudate!

Son and Mother

How many nails pierced the cross's wood
Four.
One and one for the hands outspread,
Bone and tendon and flesh blood red.
For feet, one. One for the sign above his head—
Four to the strength of the heart-wood tore.
Four.

How many thorns crowned Messiah's brow?
Ten.
Each like the prong of an angry plough,
From which ten blooms of bright blood grew.
The color of death and of debt long due
Cancelled with ink from God's own pen.
Ten.

How many swords stabbed Mary's heart?
One.
The cry on the cross was its sharpest dart.
She'd pondered the pain from the very start
Till it grew to a life-long ache. The hurt
Weighed huge and chill as a burying stone—
One.

Slide Photography: Climbing the Mount of Olives

A grey wall fills the lens—old limestone
crowned with a branching weed
that blocks the sun (miraculous
that an herb so small can stop
the sun).
       Hugging the barrier, close
as a disciple, the steep path
creeps up from Gethsemane. The click
and the click of the defining shutter
frames rectangles from which all sounds
will die, carried away
by air and time. Like the words
on this page, slides are silent.
It is the remembering mind that hears the
Arab children's cries, crowds ancient alleys
with movement and the pungent smell
of sesame oil, calls back a vacant lot
rank with poppies red as
spilled blood.
       So how may we,
his distant pilgrims, know him real (whose
Garden presence still guards the gnarled,
secret olives)? Faith listens for his story
in the everyday neigh of a donkey,
an explosive obscenity, the threat of
armed soldiers, sweat on any dark skin,
the clink of coins, thorns pricking, metal
clanging on metal, a cloth tearing.

Listen to the Green

1955-1970

But Not Forgotten

Whether or not I find the missing thing
it will always be
more than my thought of it.
Silver-heavy, somewhere it winks
in its own small privacy
playing
the waiting game with me.

And the real treasures do not vanish.
The precious loses no value
in the spending.
A piece of hope spins out
bright, along the dark, and is not
lost in space;
verity is a burning boomerang;
love is out orbiting and will
come home.

Circles

I sing of circles, rounded things,
      apples and wreaths and wedding rings,
  and domes and spheres,
      and falling tears,
  well-rounded meals,
      water wheels,
    bottom of bells
     or walled-in wells;
  rain dropping, golden in the air
        or silver on your shining hair;
    pebbles in pewter-colored ponds
      making circles, rounds on rounds;
  the curve of a repeating rhyme;
    the circle of the face of time.
Beyond these circles I can see
      the circle of eternity.

Does passing of each season fair
      make of the four a noble square?
  No. For to each the others lend
    a cyclic, curving, rhythmic blend.
  Remember, spring in summer gone
      comes round again. New spring comes on.

      The circle in the eagle's eye
    mirrors the circle of the sky,
the blue horizon, end to end,
      end to end,
     over earth's never-ending bend.

The arc of love from God to men
      orbiting, goes to him again.
    My love, to loving God above,
      captures *me* in the round of love.

Rib Cage

Jonah, you
and I were both signs
to unbelievers.

Learning the anatomy
of ships and sea animals the hard way—
from the inside
out—you counted (bumping your stubborn head)
the wooden beams and the great
curving bones
and left
your own heart unexplored.
And you were tough.
Twice, damp but undigested,
you were vomited. For you
it was the only
way out.

No, you wouldn't die.
Not even burial softened you
and, free of the dark sea prisons,
you were still
caged in yourself—trapped
in your own hard continuing rage
at me and Nineveh.

For three nights
and three days dark as night—
as dark as yours—
I charted the innards
of the earth. I too swam
in its skeleton, its raw underground.
A captive
in the belly of the world
(like the fish, prepared by God)
I felt the slow pulse at the monster's heart,
tapped its deep arteries, wrestled

its root sinews, was bruised
by the undersides of all
its cold bony stones.

Submerged,
I had to die, I had
to give in to it, I had to go
all the way down
before I could be freed
to live for you
and Nineveh.

Slow Passage—Teel's Island*

Though now you ride the crest of the field
and rise to the seasonal
slow heaving of the earth,
the gulls are the same, and the
restless sky.
Under you, strong airs still push
the waves—salt grasses lifting darkly
to break in milkweed, yarrow, queen anne's lace.

Never, now, dolphins. Moles
are the travelers in your deeps.
Field mice and crickets dart
among the weedy shallows at your stern.
Lichens barnacle your beam.
Only the rains wet your grey shrunken wood.
Only wind slaps your sides.
The far barn's lightning rod
is the lone compass needle
to tell you your true north.
And oars I cannot see
pull, twist and feather
in your stiff rowlocks, to keep you
heading west.

Teel's Island is the title of Andrew Wyeth's painting which
shows an old dinghy stranded high in a field.

Bride

The thin smooth eggshell of her
   rigid, indrawn by private gravity—
   her convex surface
   offers no toe-hold for analysis.
But perhaps the perfect smile—
   the self-assured sheen—
   her insularity's bright
   white carapace that shuns another's touch
   ask of you:
Is it her coolness or her cowardice
   (or are they one) that closes in-
   ward on itself
   denying entrance?
The probes of God's sharp grace
   his bruising mouth (and yours)
   threaten to broach her brittleness.
   And heaven's breath, hot,
   see how she shrinks from it
   on her ice palace
   as from all passion that seeks
   center
   in her hidden hollowness.

Not knowing she's destined for shell
   shock
   vainly she shields her vulnerable vacuum—
   postpones the breaking and entering—
   love's emptying of
   her chilly emptiness.

Shine in the dark I

From a dark dust of stars
kindled one, a prick of light.
Burn! small candle star,
burn in the black night.

In the still hushed heart
(dark as a black night)
shine! Savior newly born,
shine till the heart's light!

Shine in the dark II

Into the blackness breached with white
the star shivers like a bell.
God of birth and brightness
bless the cool carillon
singing into sight!
Plot its poised pointing flight!

Dark has its victories
tonight, in David's town.
But the star bell's tongue
trembles silver still
in your felicity.

Shine in the dark III

The stars look out on
roofs of snow.
They see the night,
a velvet glow
with amber lanterns
shining so.

God searches through
the sweep of night.
Is there a heart burns
warm and bright
to warm God's own heart
at the sight?

to the municipal incinerator

among the perishables, go the
things of value, the shining cans, the plastic
forks, the occasional
alarm clock, assorted galvanized nails,
doll carriages, and dolls with most of their hair
left, machine parts and of course
odd shoes, applecores with sweet flesh on them,
frilled escarole, bones,
lobster shells, cartons, ashes, peelings, the decay
trapping the unspoiled parts, the untouched,
unused garbage of our lives, committing all
the lovely leftovers of affluence
to the sanitary engineers —
strong string, umbrellas of nine good spokes,
spools (naked but solid, clean, functional)
socks with only one hole, magazines
four weeks old and full as ever of wisdom and fact
and startling color,
cologne bottles of perfumed air, clear
as ice and less disposable,
and, in early January, Christmas trees
bared of everything but themselves,
and crumpled golden gift wrap—a bright heat
lying in wait for kindling

how many poets, soul
singers,
how many souls, how many brothers, how
many glistening minds, how many bodies,
how many eyeballs, hands, arms, quick black
feet, potent loins, fertile wombs, voices,
sinews, agile tongues, smoldering hopes,
hearts, proliferating brains
rot in the city?—refuse shovelled into
the disposal system, bound for some hot fire out of
sight out of mind—

refuse—I have refused you.
I have habitually ground
the dirty orange peel of your indignity under
my heel, and cursed you for littering
my mind's landscape

words were always my undoing
and now I have committed allegory:
looking for beauty in my own trash can
my God, I found truth

The Flounder

The flounder, (destined by birth to live and lie
miming the murky bottom of the sea
unlike the weathered fisherman, and me,
who much prefer the bottom of the sky)
jerked, raised resisting from its ocean bed
dark slabbed, a wet convulsion in the sun,
gills gaping, new existence but begun
will lie soon, on the gold beach, slimy dead.

And would another angler contemplate
hooking and drawing some defiant soul
up to eternity's unfiltered glare
swiftly, in that rare air, to suffocate,
blinded and gasping, helpless on heaven's shoal,
smeared with the scum of alien atmosphere?

Royalty

He was a plain man
and learned no latin

Having left all gold behind
he dealt out peace
to all us wild men
and the weather

He ate fish, bread,
country wine and God's will

Dust sandalled his feet

He wore purple only once
and that was an irony

Bloodcount

I

In summer the grey and amber
plasma of flying insects
sprays our windshields.
Milky blood of flowers drips
wet from their cut stalks. Maples
are cupped each spring for their sweetness.
Cactuses may be bled, too: a green gore,
a drink in the desert.
Not yet content, we tap our underground,
pick at dry veins in the dark, loosen
the black and silver clots,
pockmark the wilderness with wells
and unstop gushers to relieve
the hypertension of a continent.

And watch today's ghettos!
Look at all the gutters and gibbets of
revolutions. See the startling
color of death
at abbatoirs and all the battlefields!

The medieval medics did it often,
wiping away, maybe, as they sponged
the leechwounds
the thought of a bloodletting once done
in slow stages:
lash and thorn and nail and spear.

Look back further. Smell
the holiness of ancient altars, basalt piled
and varnished with sacrifice, drops
dried to a precious enamel over gold,
flecking even the feathered cherubim
while slaking
the thirst of justice between them.

Notice the smeared levitical hands,
the thumbs and the great toes of Aaron.

Think of the blood of the dead boys of Egypt.
Think of the dead men of Egypt: their blood
bottled within them, cool under water.

Now search
old doorposts and lintels
delicately patterned with hyssop
a sprinkling that signalled not revenge
but grace, printed in
indelible lambs' ink.
The evidence spoke once for Abel.
We listen to it
still.

II

How well chosen wine was
to stain our souls with remembrance!
He knew
how it burst, vivid,
from the flushed skins of grapes
grown for this sacramental crushing:
a shocking red, unforgettable as blood
a rich brew in the cup, a bitter
burning in the throat,
a warmth within
chosen well to etch on our lintels
the paradoxes of
a high priest bound to his own altar,
death as a tool of love,
and blood as a bleach.

Blindfold

When someone
pulls down a blind
shuts out seas
sky shore
other ships
shape
of the sun (though
warm still soaks down
blanket filtered)
floats a milky cataract
over every eye:
invisibles thrive and
foghorns celebrate.

In fact, unblunted
the overlapped
bass warnings
shaking the drenched air
above soft
incessant water-lap
sound doubly close
advertising their
unseen omnipresence
as though a new trans-
parency has settled
with fog
into all our ears.

new birth: heart spring

often after easter
last summer's deep
seeds rebel
at their long frozen sleep
split, swell
in the dark under
ground, twist, dance
to a new beat
push through a lace of old
pale roots

invited by an unseen heat
they spearhead up, almost
as though, suddenly,
their tender shoots
find the loam light
as air
not dense, not sodden cold

I saw a crocus once
in first flight
stretching so fast
from a late snow
(a boundary just passed
a singular horizon close below)
the white cap melt-
ing on its purple head

such swift greening of leaf wings
and stalk was clear celebration
of all sweet springs
combined
of sungold
smell of freshness, wind

first-time felt
light lifting, all new things
all things
good and right and all the old
left behind

No backtrack, old Hansel

Age is a wilderness where your skills
   and your dry wit seem not enough
to find a path on pathless hills.
   Behind, you leave such fragile stuff—
such a sparse trail of shining stones
   shown by time's black birds to be bread
for scavengers. And no blank bones
   mark where your unfleshed dreams lie dead.
Nothingness is the harsh rebuff
   and age the wilderness where your will
and withered wit seem not enough
   to find paths on this pathless hill.

sonic boom

after this I'll be more careful
about stone-throwing in ponds—
specifically a small purple
one where even drowning gnats
make circles on the silver,
shaking its shallowness,
reaching its rim, swaying
the water weeds
who-knows-how-many
microscopic molds
spread in the sun, on stumps, submerge?
how many algae, shredded, sink
to green slime?
what trauma follows
for a water flea,
one pebble-flung catastrophe?

too much to ask

it seemed too much to ask
of one small virgin
that she should stake shame
against the will of God.
all she had to hold to
were those soft, inward
flutterings
and the remembered sting
of a brief junction—spirit
with flesh.
who would think it
more than a dream wish?
an implausible, laughable
defense.

and it seems much
too much to ask me
to be part of the
different thing—
God's shocking, unorthodox,
unheard of Thing
to further heaven's hopes
and summon God's glory.

night through a frosty window

galaxies glisten
across glass

the constellations
crowd between
clustered frost beads
tangle in their
ice-bright fringes

inches from my face
sealed-in stars
play with the planets

two kinds of tingling light
touch fingers
kiss in my eye

focusing
near to far
to near
tells me
they are worlds apart

but
melted by a breath
see
again
now they all swim together
on the dark pane

Parabola

Yes, I am comfortable
here in the dimness
almost as quiet as a
quiet nursery.
This softened oblong's
white-satin-quilted
safe as a bassinet.
Hopefully you
have swaddled me here
against time and the chill,
cradled my old age
here in the hush of
the organ lullaby.
Are you afraid that
I'll waken and cry?
Like seventy years back
(when I was new
and you celebrated
my coming. Now
my going's the theme
for your congregation).
Once more the heads
come over me, bending,
bunched and curious,
your comments, echoes—
"He looks so peaceful."
"—so like his father."
Do you think in this sleep
I'll waken? Listen—
I can't cry an answer
or cry to be lifted
or cry for feeding.
Listen—my stillness
says clearly enough that
my soaring's over
my weightless flight
in the hot white air

is done. My bird bones
will splinter, will split
in the hard earth after
such a bold arc.
You thought I was going
up forever?
But gravity claims us
each, today.
My moving parts are
all stopped cold.
I am almost fetal
ready at last
for final gestation.
A dark maternity
will hold me, treasured,
in this new womb.
Kiss me. My face
is still intact. Lock
my watertight lid
against your feelings,
against your flight wounds—
your own re-entry.

seventh day

Come Adam, son, mirror of myself,
  walk with me, talk, tell me
    do you see over there (your heart stirring)
  the grey dawn-dappled foals, ungainly,
    galloping down the brow of the world
  (fresh cooled with milky light, and
    frosted with sharp first foliage below)?
How startled the bird is
  at their hoofs' unheard-of thunder!
She springs unthinking
    into her first fine tentative lonely flight
  splitting the unwinged space
    beyond this perfect hill.

And Eve, as the clean mist unveils
    the unscarred grassy slope,
    distills, drips fragrant from the twigs
  to water the primeval greenery,
    do you smell now, on the warm-breathing breeze
  the fertile flavors of my undepleted earth?
  damp subtle essences of unploughed plains?

Listen, you two, gathering bunches from my heavy vines
  (purple and green and swung from tender stems
  with fragile bloom unrubbed)
    do you hear ground-hogs rooting happily
  in the rich undergrowth?

Below you, down a dustless avenue of oaks
  greenwashed as this first spring
    cool runs the river. Does it delight you both
  poured from my palm into my finger's furrow?
Up through the water shines the unmined gold
    and the thin silver slivers of the fish.

But here and now on your mid-morning hilltop,
  innocents, touch

each other's hands, hold, yield yourselves together
and fulfill
the ardent rhythm of the sun.
Bathe in the blue aisles of light over you
and in them feel the farthest reaches of my love
and urgent joy, in you.
Laugh with me! Join in my delight!

Now rest
under my hand, which also rests today.
For your strong answering pleasure in my toil, my
touch, is my contentedness.

The celebration

We might well
feel sorry for the
elder brother.

All he gets for his pains is
promises—promises,
a firm reproach, a truthful telling
that virtue brings
its own reward
while in the ballroom
across the hall
the black sheep and all his
loud friends
think it a fine Homecoming,
dance, laugh, live it up.

The firstborn's lack is
he's only a brother.

He hasn't tasted
parenthood, hasn't learned
the hard way
that love, longing,
endurance, disappointment,
bitter concern
often flower in stronger love
and later,
a more merry heart.

We would hate
to wish it on him, but
he can understand
only if, someday, *he* has
a prodigal son.

Under the snowing

Under the snowing
the leaves lie still.
Brown animals sleep
through the storm, unknowing,
behind the bank and the frozen hill.
And just as deep
in the coated stream
the slow fish grope
through their own dark, stagnant dream.
Who on earth would hope
for a new beginning
when the crusted snow
and the ice start thinning?
Who would ever know
that the night could stir
with warmth and wakening
coming, creeping,
for sodden root and fin and fur
and other things lonely and
cold and sleeping?

common ground

new dug, rail braced, young ash blond
fence posts span the frozen slope
wedlocked in pairs repeating down
the road and out of sight
but there's an older couple
sharing the upper view across the river
(he's beech, she's thorny
bramble) whose tops feather today's
frost fog, whose ranging roots
lodge interlaced in the lean soil
that also anchors milkweed ragweed
thistle sorrel dock
time tangled the two (branch
and toe touched, leg locked)
season shift and shadow color them
alike, green gold or grey
rain rinses them
westerlies bare their brows
snows sift over their stiffness
and a bleached spring sun
speeds their slow sucking
from a common spring

Perfect love banishes fear
1 John 4:18 (NEB)

The risk of love
is that of being unreturned.

For if I love too deep,
too hard, too long
and you love little
or you love
me not at all
then is my treasure given,
gone,
flown away lonely.

But if you give me back
passion for passion,
return my burning,
add your own
dark fire to flame my heart
then is love perfect
hot, round, augmented,
whole, endless, infinite,
and it is fear
that flies.

Small song

God of the sky,
God of the sea,
God of the rock
and bird and tree,
you are also
the God of me.

The pebble fell.
The water stirred
and stilled again.
The hidden bird
made song for you.
His praise you heard.

You heard him sing
from in the tree.
And searching still
I know you'll see
the love that wings
to you from me.

Of consolation

It is down
makes
up seem
taller
black
sharpens white
flight
firms earth
underfoot
labor
blesses birth
with
later sleep

After silence
each sound
sings
dull clay
shines the
bright coin
in the pot
lemon
honeys its
sweet sequel
and my dark
distress
shows comfort
to be doubly
heaven-sent

Moses reclothed

Bare-soled he waits,
bowed bare-headed, stripped to the heart,
eyes narrowing, hands to his face
against the heat,
watching

Hissing, the dust-dry leaves
and cobwebs shrivel
baring the thin curved thorns
woven with gold
and the black-elbowed branches
wrapped in a web of flame
(An incandescence brighter
than the burnished mountain
under the burnished sky)

Wondering he waits
in the hot shadow of the smoking voice—
observes no quivering flake of ash
blow down-draft from the holy blaze
none glowing on the ground—
Shrinking, himself, before the scorching blast,
he sees the unshrinking thorny stems alive
seared but still strong, uncharred
piercing the fire

Enveloped now in burning ardent speech
he feels the hot sparks touching his
tinder soul
to turn him into flame

A song for simplicity

There are some things that should be as they are:
plain, unadorned, common and all-complete;
things not in a clutter, not in a clump,
unmuddled and unmeddled with;
the straight, the smooth, the salt, the sour, the sweet.
For all that's timeless, untutored, untailored and untooled;
for innocence unschooled;
for unploughed prairies, primal snow and sod,
water unmuddied, wind unruled,
for these, thank God.

Singly and strongly, from each separate star
a brightness pricks the retina from far
to near. And for clear eyes to see
deep space and dark infinity
with an untroubled gaze,
give praise.

With both hands unjewelled and with unbound hair
beauty herself stands unselfconscious where
she is enough to have, and worth the always holding.
The mind perceiving her, the heart enfolding
echoes the unchanged pattern from above
that praises God for loveliness, and love.

Glory again to God for word and phrase
whose magic, matching the mind's computed leap,
lands on the lip of truth,
(plain as a stone well's mouth, and as deep)
and for the drum, the bell, the flute, the harp, the bird,
for music, Praise! that speaks without a word.

As for the rightness to be found
in the unembellished square and the plain round,
in geometric statement of a curve
respond! without reserve
but with astonishment that there's for every man

one point in time, one plainly drafted plan,
and in your unique place
give glory for God's grace.

All this from him whose three-in-one
so simply brought to birth
from the red earth
a son.
All our complexity, diversity, decor
facet the gem, encrust the clarity.
So pierce you now the opalescent glaze
till all your praise
rises to him in whom you find no flaw.

Of elms and God

A glib wind sings.
Wide blowing branches
are gravid with damp buds
dropping thin
brown hulls like insect wings
into the choked gutters
and warm airs and showers
are smudging winter's hard-
etched edges
fuzzing the dark wood skin
with pale and pendant flowers
until the twigs are diluted
to the color of fog.
And now, all my green
thoughts about elms in spring—
a tender catalog—
are drawn together, seen
in this one tall and lovely thing
rooted in my door-yard sod.

Yes, it is easy enough
to talk about an elm, but how
do I find words for God?
Spirit is not so readily trapped
in parts of speech
and to evaporate him to an abstract
is too simple, and not safe.
My verbal reach-
ings for him, like worn and
cast-off clothes, fit
him badly. He escapes them
undefined. They are not filled.
He is not found.
But if God sent to me
one signal from

himself—
if he distilled
his deity—
I would be bound
to take his Word for it.

Exit

When you go will you
go with a sizzle—
a spiteful spitting on a
hot plate,
a jig of steam?
with a crystal sigh on a beach
to leave a bubble?
or will your trickle
run, thinsilver,
to the open ocean?

When you leave will you
leave with a bang—
exploding like a
far star,
kicking your
hot cinders in God's eye?
or quietly, clinging
to your black match-stick corpus
a slow blue shrinking
in the dark?
or will your bud of burning
lift, bloom bright,
to a wider light?

". . . for who can endure the day of his coming?"
Malachi 3:2

when an angel
    snapped the old thin threads of speech
        with an untimely birth
    announcement, slit
    the seemly cloth of an even
        more blessed event with
  shears of miracle,
    invaded the privacy of a dream,
multiplied
    to ravage the dark silk of the sky, the
        innocent ears
      with swords of sound:
news in a new dimension demanded
    qualification.
The righteous were as vulnerable as others.
    They trembled for those strong
    antecedent *fear nots*, whether goat-
      herds, virgins, workers in wood or
        holy barren priests.

in our nights our
    complicated modern dreams rarely
      flower into visions. No
    contemporary Gabriel
    dumbfounds our worship, or burning,
    visits our bedrooms. No
  sign-post satellite hauls us, earth-bound but
  star-struck, half
    around the world with hope.
Are our sensibilities
  too blunt to be assaulted
    with spatial power-plays and far-out
    proclamations of peace? Sterile,
  skeptics, yet we may be broken
    to his slow silent birth

   (new-torn, new-
    born ourselves at his
     beginning new in us).
His bigness may still burst
    our self-containment
   to tell us—without angels' mouths—
fear not.

God knows we need to hear it, now
    when he may shatter
    with his most shocking coming
   this proud cracked place
and more if, for longer waiting,
  he does not.

Two answers to poverty

Along strict curbs and
over the cautious grass,
generously
the layered leaves are flinging down
a thousand polished keys
to their silvery city.
Choose one. (Each holds
the shining secret of maple trees.)
Turn it in its dark lock
for future fortune. Now
it glows in one bright thought
but, come autumn, its opulence
will ransom some of us.

The grass is captive.
How can it fill a city
with sun's splendor?
And dandelions (spring's
most useless bounty, but
lovely for glancing)
gave away all their coins and got
toothless old age for it.
Pick one. In the grey beard
is gold. Mind blows it away
but next year
the yellow millions
will glitter for you too!

Arrested

"All crossroads have given way to cloverleafs. . . ."
—Thomas Howard

In this chase
only he
knows all
the ins and outs.

I am so used to
crossroads—I
who always like straight-
forwardness, accepted
confrontation
and other absolutes,
trusted all traffic lights
submitted to speed limits
responded
to the red octagonal STOP
and stopping
believed the old road markers
pointing, plainly,
both ways.

I who never minded on-coming
cars, I who lowered my
headlights dutifully,
find no felicity
in these new
concrete convolutions.
Risk is behind their
black banked pavement.
The subtleties
of multi-level loops
and one-way curves
go to my head in a blaze
of slick, a foliated
whirl of orange vertigo.

Fore and aft are irrationally
punctuated
with directional signals and
quick implacable squares
that shout NO STOPPING
and other orders I am going
too fast to stop anyway
faster than decision
and on this cloverleaf
luck has left me
alone in a snake of flight
over and over this
complex, evading
the straightaway
until his flashing eye comes
at me, up a ramp, catches me
near the sign that says
to him NO ENTRANCE,
EXIT to me.

The revolutionary

Do you
wince when you hear his name
made vanity?

What if you were not so safe
sheltered, circled by love
and convention?
What if
the world shouted at you?
Could you take the string
of hoarse words—glutton,
wino, devil, crazy
man, agitator, bastard,
nigger-lover, rebel,
and hang the grimy ornament
around your neck
and answer
love?

See the sharp stones poised
against your head! even
your dear friend
couples your name with curses
("By God! I know not God!")
the obscene affirmation
of infidelity
echoes, insistent,
from a henhouse roof.

Then—Slap! Spit! the whip,
the thorn. The gravel
grinds your fallen knees
under a whole world's weight
until
the hammering home of all
your innocence
stakes you, stranded,

halfway between hilltop and heaven
(neither will have you).

And will you whisper
forgive?

Mary's song

Blue homespun and the bend of my breast
keep warm this small hot naked star
fallen to my arms. (Rest . . .
you who have had so far
to come.) Now nearness satisfied
the body of God sweetly. Quiet he lies
whose vigor hurled
a universe. He sleeps
whose eyelids have not closed before.

His breath (so slight it seems
no breath at all) once ruffled the dark deeps
to sprout a world.
Charmed by dove's voices, the whisper of straw,
he dreams,
hearing no music from his other spheres.
Breath, mouth, ears, eyes
he is curtailed
who overflowed all skies,
all years.
Older than eternity, now he
is new. Now native to earth as I am, nailed
to my poor planet, caught that I might be free,
blind in my womb to know my darkness ended,
brought to this birth
for me to be new-born,
and for him to see me mended
I must see him torn.

to know him risen

Is it obliquely
   through time's telescope, thick-
   lensed with two thousand Easters?
Or to my ear in latin, three chanted
   'Kyries' triumphing over a purple chancel?
Or in a rectangular glance at sepia snapshots
   of Jerusalem's Historic Sites?
Can I touch him through the cliché crust
   of lilies, stained glass, sunrise services?
Is a symbol soluble?
Can I flush out my eyes and rinse away
   the scales?
Must I be there?
Must I feel this freshness
   at an interval of inches? and sense, in-
   credulous, the reassurance of warm breath?
   and hear again the grit of stone
   under his sandal sole?
   those familiar Judean vowels
   in the deep voicing of beatitude? recognize
   the straight stance, quick eye,
   strength, purpose, movement, clear command—
   all the swift three-day antonyms of death
   that spring up to dispel its sting,
   to contradict its loss?
Must I be Thomas—belligerent in doubt,
   hesitant, tentative, convinced, humbled, loved,
   and *there?*
Must sight sustain belief?
Or is a closer blessedness
   to know him risen—now
   in this moment's finger-thrust of faith—here
   as an inner eyelid lifts?

to a young suicide

you always walked the edges
of the world
like eggshells
afraid
of your own weight

you nibbled at life
wrote novels with no
endings, dropped courses
in mid term, wore smooth
your records' outer rims

only once you
took a bite of God—and spat him out
he was more than you could swallow
like a tough rind
like all your half eaten apples

letters you wrote were never sent
(I would have read them)
often your face was censored
your laughter flat
even your dreams were incomplete

today
at last
your silence became pure
your escape final, finished
full (you can't be half dead)

for you
death offered
no samples
only this huge and
bitter pill

Hundredfold

Yesterday
(after first frost, with maples
blazing beyond fringes of stubble hay)
my husband and my sons
pulled up dead summer's stalks of corn
laying them flat among the weeds
for ploughing in again when next spring's born

I'm glad I picked the green tomatoes
two nights ago
and spread them, newspapered,
to ripen on the basement floor
good company for the corn relish, row
and golden row in jars behind the closet door

Yes, I'm very glad
something's left—something not dead
after all the hilling and hoeing
seeding and sprouting, greening and growing—
after the blowing
tassels high as a woman's hands above her head
    Corn relish for Sunday dinner—grace
    the days when outside snowings
    whiten winter's face!

Let me leave fruit
(but not in someone's basement)
when I grow browned
and old and pulled up by the root
and laid down flat
and ploughed into the ground

Absolute-ly

If roads went nowhere
and rains fell dry,
if birds crawled low
and worms flew high,
if faces were flat
and the midday sky
looked always dark
and the sun shone square,
if beauty were costly
and God unfair
if densest earth
were as thin as air,
if clocks went backwards
and grass grew blue
and lions were happiest
in the zoo
and five were the sum
of two and two
would you be me?
might I be you?

How would we *think*
if all sprouts grew down
and the sea churned pink
and the clouds turned brown
and God's face were fixed
in an awful frown?
I'm thankful, I'm thankful
(are you too?)
that grass is green
and sky is blue
and the sun is round
and fact is true
and we can count on
gravity,
and God is good

and beauty free
and, for the sake of
our sanity,
that you are you
and I am me.

"... for you are a mist"

James talked about transience.
Noticing
a spider's web under the olive trees
splendidly hung with early drops, already
vanishing up the vortex of the air
perhaps he saw there all his grandest schemes—
the purity of Israel's infant church
the apostolic councils
solemn conclaves
policy declarations and decrees—
a trivial display to heaven's wide arch
all to be sucked away
into one brilliant plan—not his.

As he saw the rain
stinging the earth into a fruitful green
then smoking, steaming up under the eastern sun
surging away in
farewell to the parching plain
he must have sensed his own stern, sturdy life
(condensed at birth under that human skin)
now gathered in him, waiting
the inevitable evaporation,
the final up-draft that would leave
his muscles dry, his strong bones prone
and his dark skull a shell.

It may have been a palestinian dew
(sparks among thirsty grasses)
showed him the simile,
or Jordan at dawn, a flowing amber
sending up a veil to blot the sun.
Did he ask himself—Christ's brother—
    What is my short span?

        a heaven-sent refreshment? or a curtain
        cutting out the light?
And I must ask it now
(small moisture that I am)
under the sun of God's great grace on me:
        Which am I—dew, or fog?

Made flesh

After
the bright beam of hot annunciation
fused heaven with dark earth
his searing sharply focused light
went out for a while
eclipsed in amniotic gloom:
his cool immensity of splendor
his universal grace
small-folded in a warm dim
female space—
the Word stern-sentenced
to be nine months dumb—
infinity walled in a womb
until the next enormity—
the Mighty, after submission
to a woman's pains
helpless on a barn-bare floor
first-tasting bitter death.

Now
I in him surrender
to the crush and cry of birth.
Because eternity
was closeted in time
he is my open door
to forever.
From his imprisonment my freedoms grow,
find wings.
Part of his body, I transcend this flesh.
From his sweet silence my mouth sings.
Out of his dark I glow.
My life, as his,
slips through death's mesh,
time's bars,
joins hands with heaven,
speaks with stars.

Step on it

All these broken bridges—
we have always tried to build them
to each other and
to heaven. Why is it such a
sad surprise when last year's iron-strong
out-thrust organization, this month's
shining project, today's
far-flung silver network of good
resolutions
all answer the future's questions with
rust
and the sharp, ugly jutting
of the unfinished?
We have miscalculated every time.
Our blueprints are smudged.
We never order enough steel.
Our foundations are shallow as mud.
Our cables fray.
Our superstructure is stuck together
clumsily
with rivets of the wrong size.

We are our own botched bridges.
We were schooled in Babel
and our ambitious soaring
sinks in the sea.
How could we hope to carry your heavy glory?
We cannot even bear the weight
of our own failure.
But you did the unthinkable.
You built
one Bridge to us
solid enough, long
enough, strong enough
to stand all tides for all time,
linking
the unlinkable.

air craft

wind is your
flight pattern

you have wings that work
and a real beak and
no wheels

you are not made of
rivets and sheet
metal: shafts of air
backbone your light
lapped vanes

floating: your straight stems
lie flat against your fan
and when you stand stiff
on sand and salt frost
they are bare
ends of the wires that
firm your flesh

you are
soft as sky and stern
as sea

your markings are
international: grey
and white for the
world's clouds and black-
tipped dark
as all stormy water

laced with lightning
you are bow and arrow both
shooting yourself
up at infinity

but your aim fails:
falling your path drops
and folds clean as a wave
I love you

the sun shines through
your edges: you have eyes
for windows and you light
lightly on this pier and
look at me
as if God made you

Coins

Straitened for centuries between his banks,
ironed smooth by the blue weights of air,
yesterday's shining river
broke again into a thousand wrinkles.
Not age, nor strain but
summer's reckless breathing
captured the careless gold
and spread it prodigally edge to edge
stolen, new-minted
from the sun, to my delight,
by rebel water, spendthrift wind.

Stiff breathless oaks
guard the flat face of channeled grey
glass, misted, docile again, blindfold
under this next morning's
stifled sky. And I'm no Midas.
All the gold is gone.
(But for a few pennies' worth of
shine I've hoarded—locked away
from the sun's claim.)

Freeway

The split sky should have been
  sign enough. Clean and unclouded, gold
  filled the east and warmed my face.
  Arching above, the slate sharp-
  fronted shadow outpaced mine, the heavy speed of snow
  only a sullen threat until
  first flecks, erratic, isolate,
  fling down a hissing challenge on the glass,
  flake faster, a bright diffusion blunting
  the asphalt edges, bleaching away
  all burning blues, muffling
  the brass coin still
  indistinctly glinting in its pouch of sky,
  thick flocking the curved crystal,
  a wall of falling stars, a flying
  fog of white and thicker white
  and white thin as a thread
  and then the grace of a grey
  shape standing, single-footed, in a deepening drift,
  brow brushed with white, as snow blind as myself,
  dumb but definitive—"MAXIMUM SPEED 65."
It might as well say 90 (or 20)
  now that there's no bite
  through to the black bone of the road,
  no boundaries, nothing but one
  half-smothered sign to show
  the shoulder-frontiers of this space
  (a valley filling up
  with furious purity,
  a splash of whitewash for the world,
  clean covers endlessly unfolding
  for my chrysalis.)
Snow blanket? stopping here to wait
  I may as well pretend I'm warm.

Ever green

topped
with an earth-bound angel
burdened
with man-made stars
tinsel bound
but touched with
no true gold
cropped
girdled with electricity
why be
a temporary tree
glass-fruited
dry
de-rooted?

when you may be
planted with purpose
in a flowered field
and where
living in clean light
strong air
crowned with the repeated gold
of every evening,
every night
real stars may nest
in your elbow
rest
be found in your shade
healing
in your perennial green
and from deep springs your roots
may suck enough to swell
your nine sweet fruits

Triptych

The sun shines through you
splashing your primary
color hot all over
the altar and the pews
stamping the prim, primitive
shadows of your Passion
on the bare wood

Christ—you
and your Apostles
are up there so stiff
paralyzed in the
gothic frame
their tears futile, frozen
gems in black settings—you
a captive of glass
caught by the nails and the thin lead

you who have surveyed
our centuries
with translucent benediction—
you who have been held
high and almighty
in a web of metal
your angular atonement
colorfully captured for worship
outlined for adoration—
you whose crystal halo holds no
light of its own behind the thorns—
break your two-dimensioned bars
come down to
where we are
kneeling, drenched in your artificial red

come to us out of your
high stained window

not your shadow, not your bright symbols
but yourself—
if you be Christ
come down

Reluctant prophet

Both were dwellers
in deep places (one
in the dark bowels
of ships and great fish
and wounded pride.
The other
in the silvery belly
of the seas). Both
heard God saying
"Go!"
but the whale
did as he was told.

The partaking
John 6:53-56

Bread of the Presence
was
in Moses' day
served on engraved gold plates
to you and your select few.
And in exclusive glory
one alone and lonely man
sprinkled, with fear,
the ceremonial drops that pleaded
failure for another year
to you, known then
as only high and holy—
heavens apart
from common men.

Often we taste the
granular body of wheat
(Think of the Grain that died!)
and swallow together
the grape's warm bitter blood
(Remember First Fruit!)
knowing ourselves a part of you
as you took part
of us, flowed
in our kind of veins
quickened cells like ours
into a human subdividing.
Now you are multiplied—
we are your fingers and your feet,
your tender heart—
we are your broken side.

Take now and crumble small and
cast us
on the world's waters—

your contemporary shewbread.
Feed us
to more than five thousand men
and in our dark daily flood of living
pour yourself out again!

The Secret Trees

1971-1976

Behind the walls

Along the street a new house
is going up among the trees.
The open air of Wheaton
is being boxed in there, closed off
from rain, birds, light, leaves.
Day by day another kind of space
is being defined
by upright beams of pine, narrow
yellow in the morning's sun,
sentenced to the long darkness.
Months from now, when it is all done,
I shall walk by. Where others
notice siding, shutters, paint,
I shall see behind the walls
the secret trees
standing straight and strong
as pines in the free groves outside.

Airport waiting room

Nature's wildnesses sprout
in every crowd.
Across the aisle from me
sits a man with a mushroom nose.
My sleeping daughter's ear
is a pale shell delicately
open toward the sea.
My male companion from
Ontario is an oak tree
dropping small truths
like acorns, and from here
I can see the shades of windblown hair
diverse as all the
brown prairie grass
of Kansas.

Signs of Spring

The small towns of the midwest! Even
among the green explosions of April
they are quilted to the earth, pinned
at their square corners by the
presidential decorum of Franklin,
Madison, Harrison, Lincoln, Washington
and the systemic botany of Maple,
Elm, Walnut, Oak, Chestnut, Pine or
the pragmatism of First, Second,
Third, Fourth, Fifth and Main.
My mind is bursting with tulips! In a
small rebellion, which has something
to do with the season, my mind frees
from its propriety every street I pass.
Rooting up the iron stalks with their
pale rectangles, here I plant
an oval, there a star, cloud shapes
or small precious circles of violet
and topaz and cerulean blue that say
Peacock Place, Doorway Drive,
Chariot Way, Sing-a-Psalm Street,
Appleseed Avenue, Benevolence Boulevard,
Cranberry Circle, Goosefeather Grange,
Tapestry Turnabout. And, to the
mailman's dismay, I'd refurbish
the landscape and celebrate each spring,
changing the signs again!

Materfamilias

Mother tree
bald, old
with shoulders
white as
bones bleached
but still green
as a girl
where mosses
crust your south
and life tufts
some of your
knotted fingers
You cup small jays
in your elbows
wrinkle your
brown skin
to shelter larvae
and your roots
beam and buttress
marmot halls

Today
the morning mountain
is a breathless
gold, yet you
bend to an
eternal gale
You are a signal
to weather, a
signpost in time
pointing
the way the wind
went

The singularity of shells

A shell—how small an empty space,
a folding out of pink and white,
a letting in of spiral light.
How random? and how commonplace?
(A million shells along the beach
are just as fine and full of grace
as this one here within your reach.)

But lift it, hold it to your ear
and listen. Surely you can hear
the swish and sigh of all the grey
and gleaming waters, and the play
of wind with rain and sun, encased
in one small jewel box and placed,
by God and oceans, in your way.

In my living room

I have a carpet, green as outside grass.
Its short, dense, woolly blades all seem to wait
for the old hoover to mow down the dirt
and rake dead fibers, miscellaneous leaves
of lint, into itself. I almost wish
the rain would pour down from the ceilinged sky,
silver and fresh, onto this inside lawn.
Then, from the hanging corner globe, switched on,
(sun breaking through after the shower's over)
a flood of yellow sunlight might bewitch
a robin into pulling at a worm
daring to tunnel the closewoven sod.

The Groundhog

The groundhog is, at best, a simple soul
   without pretension, happy in his hole,
twinkle-eyed, shy, earthy, coarse-coated grey,
   no use at all (except on Groundhog Day).
At Christmas time, a rather doubtful fable
   gives the beast standing room inside the stable
with other simple things, shepherds, and sheep,
   cows, and small winter birds, and on the heap
of warm, sun-sweetened hay, the simplest thing
   of all—a Baby. Can a groundhog sing,
or only grunt his wonder? Could he know
   this new-born Child had planned him, long ago,
for groundhog-hood? Whether true tale or fable,
   I like to think that he *was* in the stable,
part of the Plan, and that He who designed
   all simple wonderers, may have had me in mind.

moonset

thinsilver as
a wish still born
she slides down
sky slopes—sits
on the sea

her mouth is wet
drinking—she slips
under—horizons
drown her bright
forehead

grandmother's arthritis

after all
her house is
full of useful legs
(chairs tables
beds) that
can't walk
and arms stiff
as boards

Image

I have written
a finger
and the
delicate bone
of a wrist

perhaps
someday
I will be able
to show you
a torso

Convention

Entombed at night
in the geometric, bright-
ly impersonal room
on the fifteenth floor
under a painting
that knows nothing
of art (better maybe
than the bare wall?)
I stare at the other
rectangle's gray flicker
between the curtained
window and the
repetitious mirror
lying alone
queen-sized and
unhusbanded, nor wakened
by small sleepwalkers.
The bored hum
of the air-conditioner
flattens out my nights.
It is a room that by
some cool invisible
magic picks itself up
daily while I'm gone:
the wrinkled bed
resolving itself into
neatness, the furnishings
easing, automatically
into place. Damp towels
vanish, reappear
dry, flat, foursquare.
Breakfast is achieved
at a finger's dial.
It will all be redeemed
by the end of the business,
the plane home, the
explosion of dog and

children at the door;
the roughness of a dozen
reaching arms; a chaos
of clothes in the hamper;
the relief of love renewed;
an almost empty
refrigerator
and nothing automatic
any more.

Winter wheat

Even the oaks
are almost naked.
The fall flames of rose & gold
have died out under
the dark rains.
The ground underfoot
is rimed with the cold ashes
of the wind, the bleached
stubble, the clotted
weed-heads.

But see,
over there, like a
green wound in the shoulder
of the hill, like a new patch
in the quilt,
blazes a square of quite
improbable emerald.
With what audacity
the bright velvet assaults
our autumn senses:
each blade a reversal
of seasons, its upstart shoot
flagging the brief sun bursts,
the sap juicing to its tip,
ready, now, in November,
for the new year!

The oaks are bare.
The sky is heavy with
first snow. But my rebel blood
beats higher now
against the winter night
coming.

Salutation
St. Luke 1:39-45

Framed in light,
Mary sings through the doorway.
Elizabeth's six month joy
jumps, a palpable greeting,
a hidden first encounter
between son and Son.

And my heart turns over
when I meet Jesus
in you

To Clyde S. Kilby
on his 70th birthday

It is a time when apples ripen,
friendships thicken,
maples kindle a Fall fire
west of Blanchard. Through the halls
scholars and students quicken
at a familiar voice,
and on the corner of Washington and Jefferson
squirrels and sparrows rejoice
because you're home. Like a hobbit
come back to the Shire
you're home again, our friend,
bringing Martha with you, and sunflower
seeds, a sackful of nuts, three score
years and ten worth of wisdom, under
your arm—letters and Lewis-lore—
your mind a well of wonder.

It was your mind, your inner eye, that
saw it long before it happened—
the hierarchy of shelves
dusted obliquely by the late sun
behind old glass
in the narrow room once occupied
by a minority of one
and now inhabited by Inklings and Elves.
Like a gardener raking grass,
piling the bright and varied leaves,
from far you gathered treasure, sheaves
of manuscripts, papers ornamented
with the rich, crabbed, English script,
searched out the volumes
burnished and precious with
scholarship and age—

"fact shrunk to truth" speaking
from every page.

Then you swung open for us all
the wardrobe door,
pushed us farther up and farther in
(accompanied by some favorite talking beast)
to Middle-earth, Narnia, and the Utter East.
In there, for us to re-explore,
is perfect Perelandra.
Treebeard is growing up the cornered wall.
In the Deep Space behind the rows of books
eldila elude us; Curdie
encounters Mr. Bultitude the bear.
There in that room
we smell the past, untainted by decay or death
but fragrant, for in there
the mallorns bloom
and all the blessed air
is warm with Aslan's breath.

Under the skin

The wind is rising. The golden air
wears at us, lifting the loose hairs
from our heads. Invisible waves
sweep off the grains of skin lying
like sand along the beaches of our backs.

And the sun grinds on,
a hot eye boring into all centers,
vaporizing a hidden pool, shrivelling
initiative, dissolving the wax
of the soul after the body's gone.

An infinite silence whittles away at all sound.
Colors vanish endlessly, like burst bubbles,
like small, innumerable fires gone out
under the round white weight
of a universe too grand for its diversities.

The atmosphere is always at work
polishing at untidiness: all thin
extrusions from the skull of consciousness;
the purple shadows on this planet's chin.
How easily eternity vanquishes the minutes!

Though the burnishing never ends, across
the buffeted skin of earth and man
still sometimes grows a struggling green.
Caught in the gale of space, we may yet discover
what lies behind any individual face.

ascending

for the time
being / the dark earth
was enough
to substantiate you
in our vision

but the universal circle
claimed you / rid
of a finite foothold
you lifted / scattered
your feathers in light
faceted the invisibilities
of thin air / time & space
after the light-ning
melted in one

blinded / our eyes
turn inward
so we find
your closer paraclete
our truer view

On reading a travel magazine

The phoenix' decorative flames
are about to be extinguished in a
surfeit of holy water. The Ganges
shimmers under my chair
reflecting the convolutions
of the unicorn's unique horn.
Bamboo shoots sprout
like green haiku from the waste
basket. I open my window.
All I can hear is the warm
Tahitian rain.

Poem finding a path

The words stick in the teeth.
Rich and boiling, ideas copulate
with syllables, generate, bubble
inwardly upward, unhindered
until they reach the traffic jam
at the junction of brain, breath, tongue.
There in the gullet they clot, flatten,
turn hard and dull. Wrong pieces
mate and will not come unstuck.
Shards of images, the sentences
stick in the teeth
or issue in an awkward belch,
disturbing the peace

unless they find an alternate
escape route. Somehow the joints
of shoulder, elbow, wrist,
present no obstacle. Along
striated nerves and muscles, the blips
of light and color dance and flow
smoothly, string themselves
on an iambic thread, slip
their enamel down the arm
via ink, assemble, establish
themselves according to their
innate poetry, form rows
and stand up to be read.

eternity seen from North Avenue
November 3

from the top of the
wet road
narrowed by
half a mile
& a steep slope
I see the gray
splay up & over
so that
for an afternoon
all space
is paved with
the same pale rain

there is
no difference
the road has
no end
the horizon
has been abolished
& what
is to stop me
from driving
up the sky?

O'Hareport: Taking off

As the frozen blueprint drops away
below, all sharp gray angles
and etched snow smudged with low fog,
I realize how large a view it is,
and to some degree true: these
spatial relationships are
more precisely drafted than
the landbound ones I am used to.
But the aerial look at an airport
is a geography of the absurd. From this
tilted height the real things are
quite invisible. Feelings, thoughts,
movements are reduced so perilously
small, so infinitely sharp, they are
turned as unreal as atoms. Do the
t.v. antennae, dark bristles on a
cityskin, transmit love or anger?
And the mushroom watertowers—
are they heavy with impatience or
smugness, waiting for the fire?
Does fear rise in the steam
from all those sooted chimneys,
a subtle pollutant? Does death
ride the robot highways? It seems
as if all Chicago may be struggling
to rise from its ice and steel
in a strictly defined chaos
to tell me some urgent reality.
The beginning of the message
buffets me like turbulence just as we lift,
beyond seeing, into the cloud castles.

Shooting gallery

How often
I peppered the walls with prayers
as round & quick
& plastic as the pellets
ready to my trigger, there,
at a dime apiece: aiming
at the painted decoys (each
wooden & safe as a pat answer)
not trying too hard
for fear of
winning
& having to lug
the vulgarity of
a useless prize
under my arm
all the way home.

Still,
it seemed an easier targetry
than shooting at live ducks
with real bullets
until I smelled feathers
& blood.

The tenacity of memory

"The vision that the eye accepts outlasts its object."

Even at midnight my lids swarm with the golden bees,
the blues clear as infinity, the greens
whose cool leaves stroke the brain.

The most flagrant of the odors of the sea
are vanished down the wind. I think of ships;
read of Le Havre; my nostrils question the dead air.

Thinking of old winters in Ontario, I shiver.
Childhood's icicles are slipping their shattered
crystal through my mind's fingers.

Though the pomegranate is finished, still
my tongue tingles.
My skull is filled with rubies.

Warm with words, my children's far throats
echo. The shapes of their mouths
kiss every view.

The Joining

after reading Charles Williams
and Romans 6

After the hours of restless
struggling through the waves
of fears, wounded, stroking against
gravity, treading water, stroking,
I choose to let go, to float
numbed, to trust myself to the words
sung across the lake: *Lay down*
your life, to trust my body to
the drifting wood—in weariness my bed,
my frame, the crux of all matters,
to which he was joined by force
but willingly, laid on it to be
what I have been
to gain my pain
(himself to drown in it).

                Thus
am I buoyed, and resting there
cruciform, new knowledge laps me
like a wave: *I* am the cross—
coarse grained and pocked with holes
of nails—to which he joins himself
(already joined to his deep baptism)
that he may join me to his strong escape,
his rising from the darkness of
this icy lake.

Anatomy of the invisible

What shape is electricity?
What does heat look like if
we have no skin? no eyes?

What stark form rises
in the black framework of
the house of our grief?

How heavy is gravity? with what
implacable patterns does it drag
at us from the earth's core?

Love is a quick rose liquid
or it may curl smokelike
around the tendrils of our minds.

Sound has color, as it pours
into us through our
two funnels of flesh.

Is light granular—a shaft
of sandgold from
beyond us to beyond us?

Or is it a bright wave
that breaks and washes clean
the old world's face?

Fear seems to fall with small
punctiliar precision like
the cold stars of winter.

But blessing comes as a strong
warm wind in the oak trees,
clear, a golden wine flowing.

Under glass

hurricane candles
Rhine wine
a seascape (with gulls)
dried grass
three minute's worth
of time
a ship model, ferns
in moss, photographs
all under glass
(showcases of
ourselves)
wait things to be
seen or saved
or savored
on our shelves

and here
behind the window-
glass of words
the poem on the page
preserves the clear
colors of a vision
displays an etched
view
the clue
to a memory, a green
thought, an intoxicant
idea,
dream wicks
to be lit
also
a portrait of the poet
at forty-six

Getting inside the miracle

No, He is too quick. We never
catch Him at it. He is there
sooner than our thought or prayer.
Searching
backward, we cannot discover *how*
or get inside the miracle.

Even if it were here and now
how would we describe the just-born trees
swimming into place at their green creation,
flowering upward in the air
with all their thin twigs quivering
in the gusts of grace? or the great
white whales fluking
through crystalline seas
like recently-inflated balloons? Who could
time the beat of the man's heart
as the woman comes close enough to fill
his newly-hollow side? Who will
diagram the gynecology
of incarnation, the trigonometry of trinity?
or chemically analyze wine
from a well? or see inside
joints as they loosen, and whole limbs
and lives? Will anyone stand beside
the moving stone? and plot the bright
trajectory of ascension? and explain
the tongues of fire
telling both heat and light?

Enough. Refrain.
Observe a finished work. Think:
Today—another miracle—the feathered
arrows of my faith may link
God's bow and target.

Spring pond

Look how the sun
lies on the low water!

Spread ripple shaped he
has lost roundness:

Light joined to the pond
in a fluid fusion.

And I, earthy,
wed now to the high Sun

Give God a new shape
to shine in.

Craftsman

Carpenter's son, carpenter's son,
is the wood fine
and smoothly sanded, or rough-grained,
lying along your back? Was it well-planed?
Did they use
a plumbline
when they set you up? Is the angle true?
Why did they choose
that dark, expensive stain
to gloss the timbers
next to your feet and fingers? You
should know—who,
Joseph-trained, judged all trees
for special service.

Carpenter's son, carpenter's son,
were the nails new and cleanly driven
when the dark hammers sang?
Is the earth warped from where you hang,
high enough for a
world view?

Carpenter's son, carpenter's son,
was it a job well done?

Pneuma

". . . so it is with the Spirit."
—John 3:8

The wind breathes where it wishes.
The wind blows where it blows.

A flurry of starlings
scatter like lifted leaves
across the dark October field
driven against
their own warm, southward
impulse: winged instinct
thwarted by
a weight of wind.

The eye of Your storm
sees from the wild height.
Your air augments the world
tearing
away dead wood, testing,
toughening all trees
spreading all seeds
thawing a winter wasteland
sifting the sand, carving
the rock, the water,
in the end
moving the mountain.

Your wind breathes where it wishes,
moves where it wills, sometimes
severs my safe moorings. Sovereign gusts—
buffet my winds with your blowing,
loosen me, lift me to go
wherever you're going.

It is as if infancy
were the whole of incarnation

One time of the year
the new-born child
is everywhere,
planted in madonnas' arms
hay mows, stables,
in palaces or farms,
or quaintly, under snowed gables,
gothic angular or baroque plump,
naked or elaborately swathed,
encircled by Della Robbia wreaths,
garnished with whimsical
partridges and pears,
drummers and drums,
lit by oversize stars,
partnered with lambs,
peace doves, sugar plums,
bells, plastic camels in sets of three
as if these were what we need
for eternity.

But Jesus the Man is not to be seen.
We are too wary, these days,
of beards and sandalled feet.

Yet if we celebrate, let it be
that He
has invaded our lives with purpose,
striding over our picturesque traditions,
our shallow sentiment,
overturning our cash registers,
wielding His peace like a sword,
rescuing us into reality,
demanding much more
than the milk and the softness
and the mother warmth
of the baby in the storefront crèche,

(only the Man would ask
all, of each of us)
reaching out
always, urgently, with strong
effective love
(only the Man would give
His life and live
again for love of us).

Oh come, let us adore Him—
Christ—*the Lord*.

vision

via dwindling snow and shining
mud, the brown crust gives back
the shimmering of
a spring heat

it is early april
but i see august

moving in the
hot air
above the corn field
(grey husks and stalks
scattered like
bones of an old harvest)
glimpse now the congregation
of bright tassels, the sheaths
swelling with a hundred
hidden kernels, the fluted leaves
flickering
like tongues of green fire

it is a perfect vision
a pentecost of spring

Power failure

By what
anti-miracle have we
lamed the man
who leaped for joy,
lost ninety-nine
sheep, clutched
the lunch fish
until they
not in our hands,
turned bread
back to stone
and wine
to water?

He who would be great among you

You whose birth broke all the
social & biological rules—
son of the poor who accepted
the worship due a king—
child prodigy debating with
the Temple Th.D.s—you
were the kind who used
a new math
to multiply bread, fish, faith.
You practiced a
radical sociology:
rehabilitated con men &
call girls. You valued women
& other minority groups.
A G.P., you specialized in
heart transplants.
Creator, healer,
shepherd, innovator,
story-teller, weather-maker,
botanist, alchemist,
exorcist, iconoclast,
seeker, seer, motive-sifter,
you were always beyond,
above us. Ahead
of your time, & ours.

And we would like
to be *like* you. Bold
as Boanerges, we hear ourselves
demand: "Admit us
to your avant-garde.
Grant us degree
in all the liberal arts
of heaven."
Why our belligerence?
Why does this whiff of fame

and greatness smell so sweet?
Why must we compete
to be first? Have we forgotten
how you took, simply, cool water
and a towel for our feet?

Stars in apple cores

Matthew 1:9, 10
II Corinthians 4:6
II Peter 1:19

You
are the One who put
stars
in apple cores

God
of all stars and symbols
and all grace,
You have reshaped
the empty space
deep in my apple heart
into a core of light
a star to shine
like Bethlehem's far-
to-near Night Sign:
bright
birth announcement
of Your
Day Star

Poet: silent after Pentecost

I who was thirsty, drank, was satisfied,
became myself a secondary source
of bubbling water—why
was my mouth still dry?

Brushed by dove's feathers
heart and winging mind—
I who had felt flight dared to ask
when will my words fly?

His burning oil from crown
to feet had covered me.
I was a torch for lighting, and for light
yet was my throat still dark.

The overwhelming rush,
the mighty wind wide-spread the blaze.
Yet from my tinder tongue
came not one spark.

Breasting the gusts of praise,
filled with the singing Word
and words, and still
no sound would come.

That Holy Breath, promised,
to teach lungs, larynx, lips
in a needed hour, told mine
until today, "Be dumb!"

Enoch

crossed the gap
another way
he changed his pace
but not
his company

May 20: very early morning

all the field praises Him/all
dandelions are His glory/gold
and silver/all trilliums unfold
white flames above their trinities
of leaves all wild strawberries
and massed wood violets reflect His skies'
clean blue and white
all brambles/all oxeyes
all stalks and stems lift to His light
all young windflower bells
tremble on hair
springs for His air's
carillon touch/last year's yarrow (raising
brittle star skeletons) tells
age is not past praising
all small low unknown
unnamed weeds show His impossible greens
all grasses sing
tone on clear tone
all mosses spread a spring-
soft velvet for His feet
and by all means
all leaves/buds/all flowers cup
jewels of fire and ice
holding up
to His kind morning heat
a silver sacrifice

now
make of our hearts a field
to raise Your praise.

. . . for they shall see God.
Matthew 5:8

"They only saw Jesus—and then but the outside Jesus, or a little more. They were not pure in heart. . . . They saw Him with their eyes, but not with those eyes which alone can see God . . . the thought-eyes, the truth-eyes, the love-eyes can see Him." —George Macdonald

Christ risen was rarely recognized by sight.
They had to get beyond the way he looked.
Evidence stronger than his voice and face and footstep
waited to grow in them, to guide their groping
out of despair, their stretching toward belief.

We are as blind as they
until the opening of our deeper eyes
shows *us* the hands that bless and break
our bread, until we finger
wounds that tell *our* healing, or witness
a miracle of fish, dawn-caught
after our long night of empty nets. Handling
his word we feel his flesh, his bones, and hear
his voice saying *our* early-morning name.

Angel Vision

Seeing Creation come, they know it well:
the stars, the shoots of green shine for them
one by one. They have eternity to learn
the universe, which once encompassing, angels
forget not. Clean as steel wires, shining
as frost, making holiness beautiful, aiming
at the Will of God like arrows flaming
to a target, earthly solidity presents no
barrier to their going. Easily they slope
through the rind of the world, the atoms
pinging in their celestial orifices. Matter
& anti-matter open before them like a Bible.
Inhabiting the purposes of God, Who is
the Lord of all their Hosts, in Deep Space
their congregation wages war with swords of fire
& power & great joy, seizing from the
Hierarchies of Darkness Andromeda's boundaries
& all constellations. The rising Day Star
is their standard bearer, as on earth they stay
the Adversary's slaughter of the Sons of God.
                              Praise
is their delight also. Rank on rank they sing
circularly around the Throne, dancing together
in a glory, clapping hands at all rebellion
repented of, or sheep returned. They who
accompany the bright spiriting up of a redeemed
swimmer from the final wave, who trace
the grey, heavy clot that marks the drowning
of the profane to his own place—how can we
think to escape their fiery ministry? We listen
for their feathers, miss the shaft of light
at our shoulder. We tread our gauntlet paths
unknowing, covered by shields of angels. (The ass
sees one & shames us for blindness.) "Fear not"s

unfurl like banners over their appearing, yet
we tremble at their faces.

                            Seraphim sing
in no time zone. Cherubim see as clearly on
as back, invest acacia planks with arkhood in
their certainty (whose winged ornamenting gilds
the tabernacle shade). Comprehending the
compacted plan centered in every seed, the grown
plant is not more real to them & no surprise.
Dampened by neither doubt nor supposition,
they understand what happens to a worm. And if
we ask—Did he please God? Did he fulfill
the Eternal Plan for worms, drilling the soil,
digesting it? & his strange hermaphroditic
replication—did he do it well? & what will
happen to his wormy spirit when he shrivels back
to soil? heavenly Beings answer instantly,
giving God high praise for faithful worms.
The archangel sees with eyes quicker than ours &
unconfused by multiplicity. For him, reality's
random choice is all clear cause & effect:
each star of snow tells of intelligence; each
cell carries its own code; at a glance he knows
from whence the crests of all the wrinkles on
the sea rebound. He has eternity to tell
it all, & to rejoice.

                          But what is this
conjunction of straw & splendor? The echo of
sharp laughter from a crowd (of men bent from
the image of the firstmade man) as nails
pierce flesh, pierces the Bright Ones with
perplexity. They see the Maker's hands helpless
against Made Wood. The bond is sealed with
God's blood. Thus is Love's substance darkness
to their light. The Third Day sweetens the deep
Riddle. Heralds now of a new Rising, they have
eternity to solve it, & to praise.

The Sighting

1977-1981

Galilee, Easter 1979

Quietly the old lake leans
against the land,
rubbing a shoulder
along the pebbles, water-worn,
sun-warm. The lips of the waves
mouth old secrets
among the reeds.
Their edges lend the shore
a small silver. Stolid,
the brown stones move a little
in the glancing light.
The wet overlap, the shaking
of the rushes' heads,
mark a continuum
of the matter.

But will we
listen and learn,
we who walk the rough border
joining the high and the
deep? Will we feel
with our feet
the narrow margin
and sense when to stand
firm as rocks, when to
dip and rise again
and wash again,
like water,
between the green slanting
stems and over
brown boulders
warm in the sun?

Signal

I'd rather be a live snake,
   sinuous, sinister, dust
   dry, but silver quick,
   the signature of an old
   sin, venomous, a target
   of boys' pebbles
than this empty lace of skin,
   this fine froth of scales,
   this coiled shadow
   of the real, this death wish
   left, paralyzed, in the crack
   of a hot rock.

odd couples

things are so often
at odds with their containers:

our cat once nested her young
in a bureau drawer

the copper kettle on the shelf
is boiling with partridge berries

my eye sips babytears that leak
over a china rim

other mixed metaphors rush
to be recognized:

that baby in the corn
crib, God in a sweaty body,

eternity spilled the third day
from a hole in the hill,

for you—a painter-plumber,
me—a poet sorting socks,

all of us, teetotalers drunk
on the Holy Ghost

The problem with reflections

In ponds, in mirrors,
my face rises like a fish.
Both reverse me
(I have never seen myself real)
but it is the pond which moves
under a tentative finger,
water wrinkled like skin.
A few seconds—it heals
leaving no scar. Gravity
irons it smooth & whole
& my image with it.
Glass, though, only smudges
at a touch, unless it shatters
beyond mending. There is
no middle way. It will not
bend. Its truthfulness
is its undoing, & mine,
leaving my splintered
likeness staring up
from all the silver
slivers underfoot. No,

I must content myself with gleams
(Narcissus had problems)
catch myself glancing,
fragmented, from the bathroom
floor, laughing from some
summer lake. How can I
be sure which is more true—to be
a cool pool, fluid, prone
to evaporation, unstable,
greenly able to laugh
at a wound, to drown a friend
& forget it? Or precise
as glass, ice brittle,
faithful & unforgiving,
so solid a silver

that a crack is forever?
Gain or lose, I'll salvage
all I can—a real view
of the sun, maybe,
in my mind's mirror—
a prism leaping through
my own transparency.

The universal apple:
In the fourteenth year, February 14

His tongue tests the waxed skin; his teeth
invade the red, crushing at every bite
a thousand cells for their sweet cider.
Without ever thinking about it, the boy knows
he is eating a way back into his feral self,
intense, white-fleshed, veined, full
of sap and seed. He is as packed with cells,
as primal, as the apple whose stalk
has dropped away, forgotten as cleanly as
his own blackened umbilical cord. Still
hungry, he sizes up another apple to juggle
in the air, to rescue from its brief,
ungainly orbit, to hold with ardor, its hard,
heart shape robust as any girl's between
his palms. Richer than a printed valentine,
the earnest crimson captures all his senses,
incarnate and incarnadine. Its wholeness
circles his own core. But curiosity
conquers esthetics: pocket-knife slicing,
jagged, along its equator, he dissects
the small planet, laying its northern hemi-
sphere back on its buttock. And there,
from the center of its gravity,
all five valves filled with secret semen,
shines every schoolboy's model for a star.

Antique Shop,
East Petersburg, Illinois

The sign: Four Rooms of Antiques
speaks crooked through the bungalow window.
Over the door the bell rings its treble magic,
an exchange—one storey's worth of cool
and stale and dim for a sky full of July
heat. "Too hot for *anyone* to be outside!"
(Multiple angles of old wood soak up
my small complaint.) "Yep, well now,
the farmers *need* all thet heat to bring
the corn up." His voice creaks like the floorboards
of all four rooms where the smell of must
shapes the space. Seatless or frayed, pine
chairs congregate in corners, climb to the ceiling.
And there are jars of loose brass buttons,
detached pearl and tortoiseshell buckles,
willow pattern worn past the glaze, brittle
coin silver spoons, empty mason jars bluegreen
as water that say Perfect and Kerr and Ball,
faded books full of mold and old truth, crystal
salt cellars $15 the set (without salt), thimbles,
also flat irons, pestles, spindles, clamps,
pressed glass piled like careless diamonds,
planes, whiffletrees, horseshoes rusting out
their good luck, old knives; shoot! hiding
somewhere in this room maybe there's a
doorknob once turned by Mr. Lincoln himself.

I choose a small, pale, iridescent glass bottle
marked Dr. Brand's New Discovery, two brass
drawer pulls and a clay crock and pay in the
kitchen—not a woman's room—overrun with
other people's treasures gone to dust, the once
new and cheap turned quaint and costly, all
the real values mixed and stacked, discarded or
saved, like old shelves in a cast iron bathtub.
Cramped into the corner beside the sink

stained with cigarette ends and coffee, he
is as antique as anything he sells. Joints
moving hard, skin varnished with neglect,
lips like knotted worms folded lower over
upper to hide the gaps, voicebox rotting like
an old camera bellows, the skull polished as a
china pitcher, this cracked bell of a man
stares at me without blinking, still enough
in his chair for someone to stick a round white
label on his elbow and write his price on it.

Theory

Some say

birds on harpsichords
plus all the time
in the world
could have sounded
the Goldberg variations

or monkeys on
typewriters
could have come out
Dante

I say

God *had*
all the time
in the world
but didn't
need it

to orchestrate us all
and write us real
in black
and white

For Grace MacFarlane—pianist
on entering a New Year

Your heart having heard heaven's
patterns of colored sound, you
have fingered them into our listening.
Spinner of song satin, your weavings
warm our naked lives, line with light
the dullest of our dreams. When you scale
ebony and ivory, all the music
comes out green.

This new year of yours—
(loomed of love, woven
with will of God)—may all
its shining length
reflect the yet-undiscovered
greens of Grace.

After divorce
for Lanney

The in-between is hard,
the mid-air, the limbo
between bank
and bank,
the long leap (legs
flailing, body un-
grounded, askew in space)
the scare
of alien air,
the interval of being
in no place,
having no where.

With love left behind,
an uncertain landing waits.
Suspended,
mind
anticipates,
feels the fall—feet first
on firm sod, or (up-ended,
unbalanced, off-guard)
slipping on a cruel
gravel. Yes.
It is the in-between
that is hard.

Fire place

"Citizens protest destruction of ancient landmark."
    —newspaper headline

In one winter evening's fire
the years vanish.

The clear, concentric rings
focused at the log's core
rise, dissolved in a dream
of smoke.

The record of a century's
weather in the woods
falls in a fine, unreadable ash.

Like death, divorce and other
violence, it is a kind of
vandalism:

who can rebuild a forest,
reclaim a heart's wood?

Gifts for my girl
to my youngest daughter, Kristin

At eleven, you need new shoes
often, and I would give you
other things to stand on
that are handsome and useful
and fit you well, that are not
all plastic, that are real
and knowable and leather-
hard, things that will move
with you and breathe rain
or air, and wear
well in all weather.

For beauty, I would buy
a gem for you from the earth's
heart and a ring that is gold
clear through and clothes the colors
of flowers. I would cultivate in you
a gentle spirit, and curiosity,
and wonder in your eyes. For use,
in your house I'd hang
doors that are solid wood
without hidden panels of air, set
in walls built of brick more
than one inch thick.
On your floors I'd stretch fleeces
from black sheep's backs
and for your sleep, sheets
spun from fibers that grew, once,
on the flanks of the fields.
I'd mount for you one small,
clean mirror for a grinning
glimpse at yourself, and a whole
geometry of windows to the world,
with sashes that open hard, but
once lifted, let in a breath
of pure sun, the smell of a day,

a taste of wild wind, an earful
of green music.

At eleven, and always,
you will need to be nourished.
For your mind—poems and plays, words
on the pages of a thousand books:
Deuteronomy, Dante and Donne,
Hosea and Hopkins, L'Engle and Lewis.
For your spirit, mysteries and praise,
sureties and prayer. For your teeth
and tongue, real bread the color
of grain at a feast, baked and broken
fresh each day, apricots and raisins,
cheese and olive oil and honey
that live bees have brought
from the orchard. For drink
I'd pour you a wine
that remembers sun and shadow
on the hillside where it grew,
and spring water wet enough
to slake your forever thirst.

At eleven, the air around you
is full of calls and strange
directions. Choices pull at you
and a confusion of dreams.
And I would show you a true compass
and how to use it, and a sun steady
in its orbit and a way
through the woods by a path
that will not peter out.

At eleven you know well
the sound of love's voice
and you have, already, hands
and a heart and a mouth
that can answer. And I
would learn with you
more of how love gives and receives,

both, with both palms open. I
am standing here, far enough away
for you to stretch and breathe,
close enough to shield you from
some of the chill and to tell you
of a comfort that is
stronger, more real,
that will come closer still.

The young girl's thoughts of birds

the young girl's thoughts of birds
flower from her head like leaves
in four directions

she is their stalk
the meanings of wings rise
in her veins like sap

four bird spirits fly
from her mind into the white air
around her

in a corona of feathers
their eyes shine like berries
like black beads rimmed with gold

their yellow beaks point
the widening compass of her inner
and outer worlds

*Written after seeing a woodcut with the same title, by
Kenojuak, a Cape Dorset Eskimo, in an exhibit of Inuit
art at the McMichael Collection in Kleinburg, Ontario.*

Cosmos

"Oh now release
And let her out into the seamless world . . ."
—"The Magician & the Dryad," C.S. Lewis

The crust is seamless. Though it shows
its scheme of cracks and geographic tracings, though
it trembles often from within or crumbles at its edges
as streams and oceans wear at it,
yet no man's ruthless stitching of a border,
no careless change of politics can wall
this earth from *that*, save shallowly. Fences rust.
Surveyors die. Markings fade on the maps.
Montagu falls in love with Capulet. Rains
fall on us all alike in autumn and in spring,
washing away the lines. The grass roots cross
and kiss under the hedgerows, telling us
we are kin.

Anticipation

I have come
more than a thousand miles

to race down to the shore
(lungs sampling the waves of air,
eyes unsatisfied all the way down
through scrub pine, beach plum,
indomitable grass) to see
the sea.

But the evening is flat—tide
out—nothing to catch the senses
but coarse sand
pocked with a late rain
and far, far, the knife edge
of the salt ebb.

The Atlantic
has never been tame. I discover,
with surprise, that I am not
as disappointed
at its non-response
as if it were rising fast,
hissing black, to my desire.

Bare Roofs

". . . though I am barren, yet no man can doubt I
am clean. . . ."
> —C.S. Lewis

Against the sky their angles lean.
Their straight, steep pitch is rarely green.
A metaphor is plainly seen:

The roofs will not accept the rain;
they let it run away again
into the gutters, down the drain,

showing the trees their splendid sheen.
It does not do to be too clean
if you have dreams of growing green.

rapture

driving: Bach
at work on FM
his final voice
unfaltering
cut off mid-
phrase

through the
windshield
sings the blue
well of sky

the finale is flying
flying
up there
still
soli gloria deo

hope redeems
my earthbound
progress: I
shall hear
Bach whole
and sing
with him
the new song
the infinite
fugue
he is working on

*At his death, Johann Sebastian Bach was composing the
final contrapunta in a set of 18 entitled "The Art of
Fugue." As with many of his musical scores it was marked*
Soli gloria deo—*"glory to God alone."*

North St. Vrain Creek, Colorado

". . . the creek rests the eye, a haven, a breast."
—Annie Dillard

Between fringed banks she mounds, breasting
over waterbottom, shadownippled, naked, skinned
with sky and aspen leaves and dragonflies,
bellying between the shining boulders, a fluid
flesh but firm with the force of her going.
From the bridge at noon the heat of his seeing
knuckles down at her. Senses jump the gap;
his eyes drink until the cool pools in his brain,
soaks down the thirsty length of him. As she
has found an interval's home in his eye, he
has discovered haven from the day's blaze
in her body of water.

Matrix

Some poems
open carefully
in a quiet mind,
like those oriental clamshells,
full of dry magic,
dropped into waterglass
to spread
the brilliant enamel of
their weightless petals,
frail, without seeds,

unlike those
random thoughts thrown
into the wind
that fall
to green places,
that die & shoot & blaze
& shiver in the high
morning, ready to write
their spores
into the next breeze.

Folly at East Brewster, June 1976

That morning, after the rain
  had turned the air as thin
  as innocence,
  I thought I saw three prayers
  rise singly
  over the shingled cottage roof
  like white transparent parachutes
  caught in the blue sea-wind
  and carried toward a vanishing point
  above the Monomoy horizon.

It would have seemed a fantasy
  but for the shred of silk, a
  gleam collapsed and shrunk to
  evening anonymity,
  found lying beside the path
  that leads down, solitary,
  to the far water's edge.

Report

"Recent studies show
there's always
a fair number of bees
that are lazy,
just loaf around all
the time, don't do
a damn thing."

Thus a reader's report in
The Scientific American
Next thing, we'll
be hearing about
reasonable mules,
awkward cats,
myopic eagles,
perfect people.

The meaning of oaks I
for Doug Comstock

It is light that tugs,
that teaches each
acorn to defy the pull
down, to interrupt
horizontal space.
And falling, filtering
through the leaves
it is rain that rises,
then, like a spring
at a sapling's heart.
It is wind that trains,
toughens the wood.
It is time that spreads
the grain in rings—
dark ripples in a
slow pond.

The oaks learn slowly,
well, twisting
up, around and out,
finding the
new directions of
the old pattern branded
in each branch,
compacting, a wood
dense enough for men
to craft into a crib
for a new born, a cross
for pain, a table
for bread and wine, a door
for day light.

The meaning of oaks II

Like the unblinded man,
see the trees walking,

See
oaks and people, planted,
rooting, leafing out,
a sign in spring, a
summershade, in fall
a glory,

But observe them
most truly in winter,
naked, elemental, precise
as bones in a hand
reaching out.

"... let him hear."
October, 1979

All
our ears are blunt,
hot-blooded. We listen
for no call.
But this is the day
the trees obey
God & the season,
line the wood, wall
to wall, with gold
leaf, facet the view,
fleck the sun's eye
with motes that
fall & fall & fall.

Less
than maple leaves,
our ears are thicker.
How can we hear him bless
the branches with
his secret word—*Down fall*
so that the still air
dances? We confess
all we can do
is cock our heads
to catch the leaves' thin
whispered answer:
yes & yes & yes.

Counterpoint: March 21
for Kathleen Deck

Bach's birthday—and as
the vernal equinox
presents herself,
the wind's gratuitous
gifts are delivered,
white, wet,
in random bursts against
the studio windows.
Behind the blurred panes
the measured felicity
of scherzo and sarabande
is sheltered from
the intemperate insult
out of the north.

Looking out is like
wearing spectacles
in the teeth of a storm:
streaked with melting
stars, the glass distorts
a landscape that we strain
to see clear.
The unseasonal
monotony of white
blunts all the sharp
crescendoes of color,
blanketing Spring's
baroque bloom
with an irrational snow.

It is Bach's birthday.
Viewing the rude weather
from the conservatory,
we glory in greener
gifts: a continuo
of order and clarity,

a music patterned for
delight, its contrapuntal
voices moving, unhurried,
through preludes, fugues
and other intricacies,
and the warm, civilized
precision of organ,
flute, harpsichord.

Remember for me

Where it was once all
birds unafraid and
wild grass and patriarchal
oaks through the window,
the developers
are sending in their
concrete armies, the ranks
of billboards.
Highways have replaced
the hidden paths.

But in the front hall
the pots of dried pods,
berries, bittersweet,
brambles, gathered
four years back
remember for me
the fires of autumn
in the fields,
the quiet rains
of spring.

Villanelle for a season's end

Autumn is here and summer will not stay.
The season cuts a bloodline on the land
And all earth's singing green is stripped away.

Our parting drains the color from the day.
The oak leaves' red is clotting in your hand.
Autumn is here and summer will not stay.

The sea fog settles. Even noon is grey.
The light recedes as though this dusk were planned.
The green of field and tree is stripped away.

We shiver on the beach and watch the way
The berries' blood is spilled along the sand.
Autumn is here and summer will not stay.

In the chill air the knotted weed heads sway.
The waves have swept our footprints from the sand.
The green of all our fields is stripped away.

See how the wind has scattered the salt hay
Across the dunes! Too well we understand:
Autumn is here, bright summer will not stay
And all earth's love and green are stripped away.

Down fall

Leaves fall and burn two ways: first
from the flaming trees, a company
of dancers in the equinoctial down-
draught to a quick, hot, sidewalk fire.

Their longer falling parallels man's
from grace: isolate, earth-bound,
frayed at all their edges, dis-
integrating, down between stems
through a sieve of roots to join
earth's small, slow, smouldering, cold,
unending fires of decay.

Does Fall go back as far as Eden?

Did Eve dance, entranced,
when the first leaves on the first oaks
turned red as wine and loosed themselves?

Did the Lord God say *Good*
to beech leaves bleached back
to primary yellow?

Did Adam rake the ground clean
and burn the leaves
after his other Garden work?

November 3
for Esther-Marie Daskalakis

Crickets
are past carding in
our summer songs.
The season
is unravelling
before our eyes, rotting
as the fabric
of the field
rots. All that is
asked of us now
is that we spin
the crumpled threads,
& weave
the filaments & fibers—
sage, burnt
umber, sapphire blue—
into a curtain for
our winter view.

Prothalamion
for Jim & Sue

How like an arch your marriage! Framed
in living stone, its gothic arrow aimed
at heaven, with Christ (its Capstone and
its Arrowhead) locking your coupled
weakness into one, the leaning
of two lives into a strength.
Thus He defines your joining's length
and width, its archetypal shape. Its meaning
is another thing: a letting in of light,
an opening to a varied landscape, planned
but yet to be explored. A paradox, for you
who doubly frame His arch may now step through
its entrance into His promised land!

Epithalamion
for John & Betsy
Genesis 2:21-23

As God removed the archetypal rib
for metamorphosis, John, so did he hone
from you some temporary joys
(from discipline he makes delight)
so that he might
give you back Betsy, bone of your bone.

And Betsy, waking from your
wife-initiation, knowing now truly,
for the first time, who you are,
remember, how, when the Lord God spoke,
that curving, warm bone woke
into a woman!

Lord, let now your word leap down
again, lift the old curse, restore
Eden, and innocence, and say once more
Good! Will you, who made one like
yourself and from that one made two,
join them in one again?

The Sighting
for Dave & Megs Singer
John 9

Out of the shame of spittle,
the scratch of dirt,
he made an anointing.

Oh, it was an agony—the gravel
in the eye, the rude slime, the brittle
clay caked on the lid.

But with the hurt
light came leaping; in the shock & shine,
abstracts took flesh & flew;

winged words like view & space,
shape & shade & green & sky,
bird & horizon & sun,

turned real in a man's eye.
Thus was truth given a face
& dark dispelled & healing done.

Cathedral

During the coldest May in memory
we drive to Salisbury. My friend
is terminal, which means
her rate of ascent is faster
than mine. As we circle the Wallops
a cloud descends and covers us,
a transfiguration that whitens
the new buds on the birches and blurs
our windshield with wet snow.

We walk the glistening black path
across the Close, circle the
Chapter House, pace the damp
gravestones that pave the Cloisters.
The heat has been turned off
inside that hollow corpus
of the cathedral (it is May) and cold
fills the huge gothic ribs. Even
the gentle light from George Herbert's
stained glass face shines silver
as ice and at Evensong the first lesson
is Deuteronomical—the Cities of
Refuge and the circumstances of sudden
death—and the second is Paul stoned
at Lystra. The voices of the choristers
lift a psalm up through the carved
clerestory, piercing our soul's spaces
with a disciplined sweetness. Yes,
their throats pattern the weight of chill
with benediction while we warm
our hands between our knees.

Outside, as the sun dies through
the thin air, the spire behind us
almost touches the sky. The snow
has melted, leaving a crystal green.
My friend is terminal. Though

we see things differently (I
cannot come with her where she is going;
she cannot wait for me) we stand
and listen as the twilight blackbird
sings clear as a choirboy
from his high, naked branch.

The foolishness of God
for Gerald Hawthorne
1 Corinthians 1:20-25

Perform impossibilities
or perish. Thrust out now
the unseasonal ripe figs
among your leaves. Expect
the mountain to be moved.
Hate parents, friends and all
materiality. Love every enemy.
Forgive more times than seventy-
seven. Camel-like, squeeze by
into the kingdom through
the needle's eye. All fear quell.
Hack off your hand, or else,
unbloodied, go to hell.

Thus the divine unreason.
Despairing now, you cry
with earthy logic—How?
And I, your God, reply:
Leap from your weedy shallows.
Dive into the moving water.
Eyeless, learn to see
truly. Find in my folly your
true sanity. Then Spirit-driven,
run on my narrow way, sure
as a child. Probe, hold
my unhealed hand, and
bloody, enter heaven.

A celibate epiphany

An apple is meant to be
flower & food & tree
& if it goes to rot
what
of its destiny?

See,
here is a woman, planned
to be manned:
lover & mother.
Single, she
is other
knowing only a kind
of atrophy
(even an apple's designed
to be admired & eaten
& climbed)
and who but God
can exorcise
the trauma of her
empty thighs?
Between his palms' dance
he twirls her brittle stem.
His fingers
touch her virgin hem.
His light shines,
lingers,
& all glories glance
upon her inward parts.
His purpose finds
her heart of hearts,
conceiving Jesus
at her core
by his most
Holy Ghost. Once more,
as with lonely Mary, he
makes of her

in her own time
& in his time, his sweet
bride, also a tree
thick enough to climb
with petals
for the eye's delight
& fruit to eat.

Judas, Peter

because we are all
betrayers, taking
silver and eating
body and blood and asking
(guilty) is it I and hearing
him say yes
it would be simple for us all
to rush out
and hang ourselves

but if we find grace
to cry and wait
after the voice of morning
has crowed in our ears
clearly enough
to break our hearts
he will be there
to ask us each again
do you love me?

Triad: Skull Hill

I Weight lifter

Three nails focus
the force of
the gravity
holding the whole
Pattern in place.
And in that
trinity of pain
he knows (knowing)
his own body load,
adds to it
the corpus
of our failure
and thus computes
the sum, the burden of
his Father's
heavy loneliness.

II Forgive them, Father

Who was he? What
were his component
parts? Body
certainly, sectioned
before our eyes.
Mind—three words
from him
carried more portent
than all
our rabbinic rhetoric.
Spirit? But that
he had already
given back.
Did we dissect him, then,
take samples of

his blood?
We did, but were
no wiser for it.

III   Shake down

His own relief
relinquished,
from the storm
at the heart
of the world, God's
grandest thunder
firms and confirms
his glory,
shakes and shifts
the ground from under
the false prince,
settles
the center cross
deeper in its place
established since
the genesis of time
and space.
God. Lightning
has already
opened the graves,
torn the hanging
barrier to the holy,
focused our sight
(*ecce homo*) on his
most lasting light.

Two stanzas: the Eucharist

Annie Dillard speaks of Christ
corked in a bottle: carrying the wine
to communion in a pack on her back
she feels him lambent, lighting
her hidden valleys through the spaces
between her ribs. Nor can we
contain him in a cup. He is always
poured out for our congregation.
& see how he spills, hot, light,
his oceans glowing like wine
flooding all the fjords among
the bones of our continents.

Annie Dillard once asked: How
in the world can we *remember* God?
(Death forgets and we all die.)
But truly, reminders are God's
business. He will see to it,
flashing his hinder parts, now,
then, past our cut in the rock.
His metaphors are many, among them
the provided feast by which
our teeth & tongues & throats
hint to our hearts of God's body,
giving us the why of incarnation,
the how of remembrance.

Jordan River

Naaman went down seven times.
Imagine it—the skin coming
clear & soft & the heart too.
But can you vision clean Jesus
under Jordan? John Baptist did,
holding the thin white body down,
seeing it muddied as any sinner's
against river bottom, grimed
by the ground of his being.

Rising then, he surfaced, a sudden
fountain. But who would have expected
that thunderclap, the explosion of
light as the sky fell, joining itself
to him, violent, gentle, a whirr of
winged pieces witnessing his work,
his worth, shaking him until the drops
flew from his shoulders, wet & common
& holy, to sprinkle the Baptizer.

Burden
Ezekiel 3:3; 4:4-8; 5:1,2

How, in the body of the prophet,
is enacted the Word
of the Lord! Ezekiel lies bound,
face forward to the besieged city,
a day for a year—
on his left side for the
stubbornness of Israel, three
hundred and ninety days, forty
days for rebel Judah
on his right—
bearing their burden, the Word
a weight like a stone
in his stomach.

So does God's metaphor approach
his purpose: Word
embodied, Breath from heaven
given bone and blood,
lying prone or walking heavily
on dusty feet; dark vision
turned to speech in a man's mouth.

Head and beard razed, hair
weighed and divided in thirds
for destruction: this
is Jerusalem,
burned, scattered, pillaged.
So is the Word become flesh.

Benediction: the grace of salt

The spring stars thicken like brine
toward their zenith; sand
in July sifts through our shoes
along the beach road, a saline pricking
between the toes at seas' edge;
across the lower field in fall each twig
& blade shines crystalline with frost;
and our lips lift to the bite, the cold salute
of a winter seasoning
as the world is salted with snow.

All the earth is white with the salt of the Lord!
Observing this, the Hebrews
sprinkled their sacrifices & their newly born
for blessing. Ancient covenants
in Israel were ratified with the holy grains,
friend bonded to friend.

Caution! the heavens are shaking again:
we taste the fine tang in the air
with tongues anxious for the sting of white
to scour our souls
& heal our bitter springs
& season us with fire.

Benedicite. O Lord
by thy grace preserve us!

Bethany Chapel

Bracketed between the first
tentative prayers, a silence fills
this place, a shadowed listening
as our separateness seeks out
the Spirit's focus for this hour
and gathers strength enough
to peer and soar
into small, shining arcs of praise
held at their lower ends
by the old hymns. Christ
in this crowd of rest and rising
humbles himself again to our
humanity; and like the sheep
(trembling in the shearer's hands)
surrenders to us once more
in quietness.

As at his dark birth and death
we had his body in our fingers,
now, again, we split the whiteness
of his loaf by turns, and tasting
his imaged life against
the cup's cool rim
we take him in.
Nourished by that final flesh,
that ultimate blood behind
the chosen signs, our God-thoughts,
seeds of worship, multiply to words.
Light flows down to us, and back,
joins us in one body of fire—
one polyphon of light now
sounding out himself—
one flame of singing
burning into being.

Postcard from the Shore
1982-1985

Seeing the shore
Wedding song for Calvin & Deborah

At ebb tide the sands are stretched—
flat, damp, written on with the rain, woven
with a warm air from the west. Stitches
from gulls' feet join dunes with sea
as the tide moves in again
and each succeeding wave spells
a new boundary in a sweeping sentence
punctuated with foam. Its drawing back
pulls a silver foil across the slope.
The film flows, thins, clouds
like a breath-touched mirror, sinks
into the body of the shore.

Your marriage is a beach—a spread
of weeds and wet edges and shells
(pink-lipped, unanchored seeds from the
sea-floor, left in the open air at
high tide, like love-notes).
Now let the seasons shift your singing
sands, let the wind lift and level you,
let water—salt, or fresh from the sky—
shape all the grainy contours
of your joining into ribs and rivulets
and pools for snails and
sea anemones. Let the roar and roll
of breakers polish the quartz and agate
in your detritus. Like gulls, move
with the movement; have no fear; the edges
of the earth, the rims of rock are a
foundation under you. You will not
be swept out to sea.

Freezing rain

Most of the things a poet has to say
are tentative, lists of foggy clues
and suppositions—an unattested version
of the way the wind breathes at night,
an essay at atmosphere, predictions
as unreliable as weather forecasts. I stab
at the truth with a pencil, sometimes,
moved too suddenly to words by the shadings
on a cloud, or its shape, shivering
at a hint of thunder (sure that it
means something).

But in the lines set down on paper
all suggestions become categories—
intuition or illusion edited to sound
like logic. Naked ideas turn assertive
in print, sharp, as intricate
as the edges of a woods in winter seen
against a black sky. The most fluid
of impressions hardens like frozen
rain. A cold front is passing over:
I hazard a guess; you take it
for reality.

to a young woman calligrapher

You are, yourself, a kind
of calligraphy;
every movement you make
writes a message on the air
in perfect and deliberate
strokes. Come to think of it,
your poise, your balance on
the balls of your feet, your
fingers' flare, the lift
of your neck, your hair—
a flowing curve from crown
to waist—the punctuation
of your glance,
all form themselves
into a smoothly-drafted
letter that leaves
the precision of your signature
engraved in our minds
even after you have
signed off.

Announcement

Yes, we have seen the studies, sepia strokes
across yellowed parchment, the fine detail
of hand and breast and the fall of cloth—
Michelangelo, Caravaggio, Titian, El Greco,
Rouault—each complex madonna positioned,
sketched, enlarged, each likeness plotted at last
on canvas, layered with pigment, like the final
draft of a poem after thirty-nine roughs.

But Mary, virgin, had no sittings, no chance
to pose her piety, no novitiate for body or
for heart. The moment was on her unaware:
the Angel in the room, the impossible demand,
the response without reflection. Only one
word of curiosity, echoing Zechariah's *How?*
yet innocently voiced, without request for proof.
The teen head tilted in light, the hand
trembling a little at the throat, the candid
eyes, wide with acquiescence to shame and glory—
"Be it unto me as you have said."

Defect

The flaw is no more
noticeable, even to me,
than a new moth-hole,
or a very small bald spot
in my fabric.

Yet when
I hold the cloth
up to the window,
the sunlight
bleeds through.

. . . but the word of our God will stand forever
Isaiah 40:6-8

All flesh is grass
and I can feel myself growing
an inch an hour in the dark,
ornamented with a lyric dew
fine as glass beads, my edges
thin as green hair.
          All flesh—
and there are seventeen kinds
of us in this one corner of the
hayfield, along with clover,
oxalis, chicory, Wild Wilber—
close enough cousins for a
succulent hay.
          Early mornings
we all smell of rain
enough to drown the microscopic
hoppers and lubricate snails
along their glistening paths:
a fine, wet fragrance, but not
so sweet as this evening, after
the noon scythe.
          No longer,
now, are the windows of air
hung with our lace, embroidered
with bees. Laid low, we raise
a new incense, and under the brief
stubble, our roots grieve.

Onlookers

*"Sickness is a place . . . where there's no company,
where nobody can follow."*
                                        —Flannery O'Connor

Behind our shield of health, each
of us must sense another's anguish
second-hand; we are agnostic
in the face of dying. So Joseph
felt, observer of the push
and splash of birth, and even Mary,
mourner, under the cross's arm.

Only their son, and God's,
in bearing all our griefs
felt them first-hand, climbing
himself our rugged hill of pain.
His nerves, enfleshed, carried
the messages of nails, the tomb's
chill. His ever-open wounds
still blazon back to us the penalty
we never bore, and heaven
gleams for us more real,
crossed with that human blood.

Permanent I.D.

I will not
prevaricate—
Truth will out.
Identity clings
like a skin. Even
at a hundred yards,
without glasses,
I know my sons in any
crowd. Every book
carries with it
the permanent odor of
its ink. The knowing
hound noses out
the track of a missing
child from all the
other spoor
bisecting the field.
Around the sheep meadow
the barbs of fence wire
carry their catch
of fleece, their multiple
clues of wool.

None of us is innocent.
Even a newborn bears
the taint of genes,
the tendency to choler
or caries. Your cheeks
are smooth and tan
(youth can look
the sun in the eye);
mine are creased
with air and time
and tears.

We are all indelibly
marked. It is impossible

to achieve real
anonymity; let that
be a warning:

Each shred of cloth
or paper, each
jeweled fish scale, each
wood splinter, ice crystal,
heart-shaped green
trefoil, spermatozoon,
speaks of itself alone
and will not be silenced.
Thus, a hair
or a smear of blood
may with certainty
be traced
back to its hero
or criminal.

God and the microscope
are not to be deceived,
will never lie. Neither
can I.

Whenever

Whenever a day's plans are aborted (like
this morning, as the blizzard closed in and
tethered us to the kerosene stove) I think
of possibilities that have never come
real—the white oak out front that would
have touched the sky if lightning
hadn't lopped it, last fall's green-blooded
tomatoes nipped by frost, the writer
who might have become my daughter-in-law.
Less obvious are the poems I may never
finish, each a fetus, waiting, wrinkled,
for an image to break the waters.

Today my world is an envelope of snow
without a stamp; like me, it is going
nowhere, caught in the tail of a dream
like the one pinched off last night by a
sudden buffet of north wind. I was
about to fly again. Now I may never know
if I can.

Arrangement in space and time

Spring-cleaning should have
rid me of them. Summer should have
gathered a fresh bunch.
But this armful of autumn
is almost as antique as the pot
that first received it—the mouth
open like an O, like the rough
circle a woman makes with her elbows
to accept a bouquet.

Brittle, the milkweed stalks break
clean as bones and show the same
straw color. Freed from time, no
seasons pump their juices,
extend their shoots an inch an hour
after rain, swell the silver
strands in their pale purses.
Like dust, timelessness gathers
on the pods and the thin, split
blades. Having lost growth,
they have achieved a kind of
immortality, there where they fill
the winter window,
spilling their tarnished silver
and some old gold.

Going to sleep in the country:
Brigham Farm

Ten minutes after the light
is out, the silence, deep as the sky
at night, is broken—the dog in
the yard begins a series of howls
at a siren in the valley. My body
is prone but my mind is bolt upright.
Mentally I pace the square room
from bed to corner fireplace, from
uncurtained window to bookcase
where a hundred volumes hold collected
pages and words, the focus of
a chronology of readers. Book titles
pair off with snatches of dinner
conversation. A character from
Dickens starts a new novel in my head.
The wide floor-boards squeak
under the invisibility of waltzing
partners. The treadle of the old
Singer moves to a slippered foot.

Then a beginning of rain surrounds
the room, the house, until its
steady purpose washes out the other
sounds. Like a candle-stump
whose flame is snuffed, my visions
shrink, settle; like its thin
signature of smoke, restlessness
moves away out the door and down
the passage. Body and mind lie down
at last, together in the dark.

Trespassers

The horizon is clear
cut: an apricot silk
stretches over the hills'
dark profile, and now
that the wind has moved on,
a crystal stillness
presses in place
every tree and blade in
the shallow valley
(our eyes are not
strong enough to prove
this, but skin feels
the weight of dusk).
In the oblique light
each leaf is layered,
green as glass, on its
singular stem. The road
moves cleanly, bisecting
the view. Fields obey
their fences; the whole
view waits for us
to make a mistake,
to tear a ragged corner.
We hesitate even
to speak, to smudge
the silence, to move
the air with our breath,
to disturb sod or stone
with a single step.

Equilibrium

The day balances itself
on the tops of the oak trees.
This morning is as unique
as all the others—the changing
configurations of clouds
to the east, the intensities
of light, the layerings of leaves,
the grass—jewelled with
a heavier dew than yesterday.
Tomorrow the same sun will shine
through the drops and the same
brindled dog will bark at a
passing car, bounding and
scattering moisture, leaving
a new trail, damp and dark
green, across the front yard.

The day moves on, steadies
itself on its foundations.
Like God, true to his own
presuppositions, it shows its
shape at all its edges. As
I walk at noon, my early shadow,
shortened, meets me again
at alternate heels, precisely,
at a calculable angle.
The driveway is washed with sun;
its gravel shines
like gold nuggets.

I bring to each day my own
inconsistency, but in the end,
predictability binds me
more strongly than change—
the resurgence of spring,
the inevitability of weeds, grass
growing back behind the

lawn-mower, the prevalence
of wind, the probability of
evening, the entropy observed
in the age-spots
on the backs of my hands.

The profligate

Conscientious in her stewardship of money,
Miss Prism cut out her new tweed suit last week—
of pure wool fabric, reduced in price for Spring
sewing, a charming, muted rose with flecks of grey
and plum. After the stainless steel pins and the
dressmaker's shears had done their sharp work,
she peeled the seven double shapes up from
the cutting board (each with its tissue twin, like
layers of skin) and approached her high altar,
the old Singer against the wall, with this,
her Lenten oblation. The leftover pieces,
perimeters of precision, she left discarded on the rug,
their weave still taut and true, their color
richly delicate. The cloth's real woolen feel
is a memory of the fields of sheep—fleeces
scoured by rain—of sweat in the shearing sheds,
of the long combing and carding and spinning
of harsh virgin fibers, of dye, darkly boiling,
soaking to the heart of the yarn, of looms
clacking and shaking, the shuttles darting between
stretched skeins. Now, at last, it has all come
to this small untidiness on the sewing-room floor.

And on Easter Sunday, Miss Prism, wearing her new
pink suit with bone buttons, a silk blouse, and
her mother's real pearl earrings, deposits
a solitary dollar in the plate for the needy.

Saved by optics*

First, you must find a chip
  of cold

that has always wanted to see,
to channel the light.
Then, with hands devoid
  of electricity,

without matches even,
and with only splinters
  of strength left,

you must carve it out—the rough
eyeball—from under the brow
  of this ice continent

and polish it between
your curved palms' last warmth
into the double convex
  of a lens,

a gem without frost or crack,
cleansed by the flow
  of its own tears.

Next, you must wait, shivering,
for the slow sun
to reach the zenith
  of his readiness

to work with you. *Now.*
Focused in the eye
  of ice

(angle it exactly,
though its chill finds each
  of your fingers' bones)

a matchless flame collects
until the concentrated scrutiny
  of light

reads the dry tinder into
a saving kindling—ice's gift
  of heat and paradox.

*In The Desert of Ice, *Jules Verne tells of arctic explorers,
shipwrecked without flame or flint, who kindled a fire by
focussing sunlight onto tinder through a lens of ice.*

Letter-press: a proof-reader's complaint

The feet of my mind run to and fro
among the stalks and stems of print,
blistered with words. Letters
are like little knives—I am raw
with the evidence. The crossings of
t's, the whipping tails of *y*'s, the dots
slung by *i*'s, and *j*'s, all bombard me
like bullets. Serifs pierce.
Punctuation lacerates: commas flip up
and gouge, brackets staple [sharply]
flesh to paper, an asterisk* pricks like
a burr. And the fangs of "double quotes,"
the skewers of exclamation! Periods,
like pebbles, trip me abruptly. Or else
I slide along the fine, slippery gravel
of ellipses . . . Running such a literal
gauntlet, by the end of a chapter
I feel I may crumble in the gutter,
my wounds blotting the words, bleeding
across the narrow margins, my skin
blanched white as the sheets of paper.

*a star-shaped figure used in printing to indicate a
reference to a footnote.*

Split screen: Naples, Florida

From the morning porch I watch the beach with clouds
through bifocals. Like an aging prophet whose vision
calls for double fulfillment—soon, and later—
my sight splits laterally. At upper level people move
along the flat waves' margin in ones and twos, bright
in their flowered swim suits and turquoise walking
shorts. Clearly transient, they are like the terns,
like the tide, moving in and out of sight. The bottom
half of the view, immediate, closer than comfort,
holds the things that must be dealt with—the peeling
paint of the railing, the clutter on the glass
table (half a danish, manuscripts, coffee mugs, books
to be read/reviewed, a sweater's half-knit sleeve,
yesterday's paper.)
                        I move my head.
Reality is re-defined and still disjunctive.
The sun moves inexorably into my shade and, through
my glasses' curved crystal, finally catches me
in the eye.

Spice

*"Despite the Queen's and Prince Phillip's many differences
(he's not keen on corgis or horse-racing, he's impatient
and controversial, she can be stubborn, prim, and
dictatorial) the marriage is a good one."*

. —Good Housekeeping

Sentimentalists, purists, and some
preachers, advocate marital absolutes—
stability, a clear hierarchy for
decision, a predictable union,
unflawed as a blank page. No wonder
it ends up flat. A truer wedding's
grounded in paradox, answers the pull
of the particular, grapples a score
of rugged issues. Like horned toads
in Eden, incongruities add surprise
to a complacent landscape.

Thank heaven you're romantic and
irascible, I'm opinionated in my
impulsiveness. Thank God we can
lean together in our failing—a rusty
trellis propping a thorned rose.

The separation

No matter how intense
our touching,
or how tender—heads
burrowing fiercely
into chests, or fingers
sure, silken—
there are no
contiguous nerves
to bridge
our bodies' gaps, no
paths of words
to join our souls.
Though each images
the other's pain or
pleasure, two
remain two.
We have been seamed,
not grafted. Though
our steps interlock,
each dances
his own dance.

Do you read into this
a strategy:
separation for
survival's sake?
See it, rather,
as predicament—
our world's ache
to be joined,
to know
and be known.

The comforting
to Maxine Hancock

She said she heard the sound
for the first time
that evening

They were walking the back pasture
to river-edge
not talking, taking in
the half-moon, breathing the
lucid silence, when at their left
a wind seemed to lift and he said
"listen" and "there they are"

And she saw that the wind-sound
was wing-sound, that a cloud of ducks
was moving the sky. Without
a cry the pulse of two hundred
feathered wings
shook the whole night

She knew then
how the Comforter had sounded—
the strong breath of his arrival,
the Spirit wing-beat
filling their ears

And knowing our need of comfort
in a dark, chill night
she folded the sound into words
in a little card
and sent it to us with her love

Faith

Spring is a promise
in the closed fist
of a long winter. All
we have got is a raw
slant of light at a low
angle, a rising river
of wind, and an icy rain
that drowns out green
in a tide of mud. It is
the daily postponement
that disillusions. (Once
again the performance
has been cancelled by
the management.) We live
on legends of old
springs. Each evening
brings only remote
possibilities of
renewal: "Maybe
tomorrow." But the
evening and the morning
are the umpteenth day
and the God of sunlit
Eden still looks
on the weather
and calls it good.

Some Christmas stars

Blazes the star behind the hill.
Snow stars glint from the wooden sill.
A spider spins her silver still

within Your darkened stable shed:
in asterisks her webs are spread
to ornament your manger bed.

Where does a spider find the skill
to sew a star? Invisible,
obedient, she works Your will

with her swift silences of thread.
I weave star-poems in my head;
the spider, wordless, spins instead.

Highway song for February 14

"Kim I love you—Danny"
                              —roadside graffito

On overhead and underpass,
beside the road, beyond the grass,

in aerosol or paint or chalk
the stones cry out, the billboards talk.

On rock and wall and bridge and tree,
boldly engraved for all to see,

hearts and initials intertwine
their passionate, short-lived valentine.

I'm listening for a longer Lover
whose declaration lasts forever:

from field and flower, through wind and breath,
in straw and star, by birth and death,

his urgent language of desire
flickers in dew and frost and fire.

This earliest spring that I have seen
shows me his tender love in green,

and on my windshield, clear and plain,
my Dearest signs his name in rain.

Mixed media
Eleuthera ("Freedom"), Bahamas

Finned, masked, body bright as a bone under
water, traced with tricks of waves' edges,
I have left land to shift into new gear. It is
like flying—weightless, floating. Thighs
slick as a seal's sides, I fluke through
colored schools of scales that turn at a flick,
glint past my foreign cheek. Or I can hang
motionless in the caves of light, clear as air.
My hands, down-branched like sea-stalks, touch
at a coral's rasp, and the pink weeds' slip
and frill.
        Having swum like a gull I long now
to crease the sea's skin, to break water,
to rise airborne, to fly, gliding easy as a fish,
to clothe bird bones, wings angled
flat as planes, plucked high, dripping,
by the lift of feathers, the balance of beak
and body, the up-trusting eye—Oh,
to be at home in the sea, and as clean
and careless, there in the fathomless sky!

Epignosis

I think to myself the name
of the bird on the front lawn—
robin—wondering how
I can hear so well in my head
the name he doesn't know
himself. Nor does he have
a word for sod, or worm, or tree
or light, yet without names
he knows each better than I
for what it is:
                    sod
for its solidity and spring
under the trident feet,
the smell of the green tangle,
the whispers to the cocked ear
of a thousand roots spreading,
or crawlers in their blind
under-tunnelling;
                        worm
for the long, thrilling, elastic
pull from the earth after rain,
the wriggle, the luscious
roundness in the throat;
                            tree
for the swell of buds as the sap
hums up its height, the launch
of its highest branches
on the planes of air;
                            light
for its slow warmth, its lift
and beckon into the sun's eye,
where words evaporate
and no names are needed.

Aurora borealis

Those leopards of the sky
whose silver eyes are stars,
they prowl and hunt and crouch and cry
among the purple bars.

The arch of heaven gleams
with paw-prints, gold and grey—
their tracks, their incandescent dreams,
the traces of their prey.

From inter-stellar space
these predators of night
slink off with pale, penumbral grace
and vanish with the light.

postcard from the shore

in a wide cloud, suddenly,
a thousand gulls lift
off the salt lagoon
into a corona
around the sun
                          they circle
the slopes of air together,
moving so easily, cleanly,
my sand-clogged ankles
ache to run
                          I am trying, now,
to tell you what it is like
but words can only
hint at this moment of
heart's dance, the wonder
of wings, the folly
of flight
                          you would have
to be with me, our heads
thrown back, our eyes full
of flashing feathers, our
eardrums pierced
with splinters of gull sound,
with audible light

Summer road remembered

head low, tongue
flagging the noon air, regular
pads reprinting
the old pattern
heading north
a trotting dog rises to mind
to signal the hot stretch
between Beloit and Madison

on the shoulder of the road
there is gravel
and a flourish of cow parsley
but mostly I see the steady
dog trot
and the corners of the mouth
pulled back for water

A feathered carol

Between fence posts the five strands of wire are strung with
twenty black birds—nervous quarter-notes perched on a musical
staff—a measure of sparrows—a score to serenade the season—
a treble obbligato—a feathered carol marked *tutti, con amine,*
presto agitato, crescendo—until the sudden *finale* of wings . . .

Note

how the hidden bird
resists translation.
Her *droo, droo,* is all
I know of her,
idiosyncratic, purling
from her secret branch
layered behind leaves
and fog. *I am myself,*
the pale treble insists;
*I will not be drawn
into your dream.*

I sit on the back porch
a long time, wooing,
winding in the sound,
listening upwards for
the meaning of doves or a
clue to clear the air
between us, before
I notice one feather
resting
on the wood step.

The collector

In our house, the first of January
heralds a resolute simplicity. No,
not just the clean calendar on the
kitchen door, nor the new date
on letters; not even the bundling out
of the dry tree with its trail
of needles to the back porch,
but a return to routine. Clearing
the Christmas clutter
signals renewal, a re-ordering;
it is a woman taking off jewelry
before scrubbing the kitchen floor.

And so I lift away the mantel's
necklace, a cedar swag pointed with
blue berries and white lights.
Down comes the rosy ribbon from
the decoy duck's neck, the holly sprig
from the antique scale (my husband
was weighed on it when he was born),
the scarlet candles, riskily lop-
sided from all December's burnings.

For myself, and for this shelf
across the fire-place brick,
I plan a chasteness free of dust
and trivia—a candle-stick or two,
a copper bowl, paired pottery crocks
to anchor arcs of bittersweet.
But with a barely noticed stealth
the wooden width accumulates
its own decor: a spindrift of screws,
shipping labels, old lists,
a brass bell turned silent—its
clapper tongue plucked out by
the root, a pulled wishbone,
a curious knot of wood, an envelope

scribbled with verse, and in April,
part of a robin's egg chipped
from the sky. Disorder spreads
so surely along the mantel piece
that by early June I feel as though
the only things I've failed
to keep there are
my New Year's resolutions.

Into orbit
for Doug Engle

Eyes wise behind their rims,
shoe-laces flying, our eight-year-old
visitor has escaped the house.
We tell him the swing was put up
wrong—the ropes not allowed to hang
loose before we knotted them
to the high branch, so that the two
descenders twist always to a
triangle, its bottom held open
by the wooden slat. He unwinds it,
seats himself, and pumps into a wide
ellipse that veers, throws him off-
balance against the trunk. Curious
still in spite of bruises, he leaps
down, counter spins the darn thing,
and spread-eagles on the grass
underneath, watching upwards as it
careens and stops and ties itself
again into a spiral tight as DNA,
tenacious as original sin.
                                        In the
swing's circling, can he see the turn,
the inward pull of self's
dark gravity, the need to push
free, fly the wind, fling out beyond
release, find his own trajectory
in an expanding universe?

April

The air is filled with south—
Breath which though soft, unseen,
Pants warm from some far tropic mouth
And mists the world with green.

Military Cemetery:
Waterbury, Connecticut

Driving—Chicago to Cape Cod
and back—twice in the same season
I see again the cemetery whose shape
had sowed itself two springs ago
into my furrow mind, when in all those

April woods life lay coiled—waiting,
sun-touched, the blood beating green under its
thawed skin. How like a flag the graveyard
drapes the hill. It patterns the slope

with rows of white. The stones stand
like winter stubble, year to year,
like ranks of weathered fingers
marking well the root crop underneath,
the bodies angled behind the steep sod,

ready to rise at a blink of the sun's
eyelid, or any sudden trumpet. Glimpsing
again the ancient burial ground
at sixty miles an hour is a summons
of sorts, a reminder of Joseph's bones:

as once they called a whole nation
out of Egypt into a promised land, so now
these hidden sleepers quicken old images,
long-dormant, brain-buried,
into a new growth, a sprouting of stanzas.

skipping stones

The words are rounded,
well-worn as shore stones—
quartz and granite and
slate smooth as an egg

my ear fingers them
until they fling and scatter
from my mind's tongue,
skipping stones
glancing in the watered
light, touching the tops
of the ribbed ripples
before they sink, singing,
pure and heavy and
true as a plumb
down to their bottoming-
out, the finding of
their final place among
the others lying along
the sea-floor of this page

The Omnipresence

Reminders flicker at us from
odd angles, nor will he be ignored;
we sight him in unlikely places,
oaths and dates and empty tombs.
God. His print is everywhere,
stamped on the macro- and the microcosm.
Feathers, shells, stars, cells speak
his diversity. The multiplicity of
leaf and light says God. Wind,
sensed but unseen, breathes the old
metaphor again. Seasons are his
signature. The double helix
spells his spiral name.
Faith summons him, and doubt
blows only the sheerest skein
of mist across his face.

Clean slate

My heart's a cove
curved to the sea's
margin. Along
the tide line
particles gleam,
randomly settled by
a sudden sigh
of salt air,
the shifting weight
of a shell.
I am swept clean, ready
to be written on
by rain, or gull's claws,
or the fingers of
waves breaking.

View from the air: North Atlantic, May 1984

It is a long melting, the edges
all blinking and glinting, sputtering
at each small insult, each slap
of waves newly-released themselves
from old borders of ice. Like razors
slicing under from upper atmospheres,
like vapor from an archangel's mouth,
like sharp dreams, like snowy vomit,
like bleached underclothes set out
on the grass to dry, like echoes
of clouds, the ice fields swim,
drifting south, drowning steadily
toward their tropic metamorphosis.

Trauma Center

It was never meant
to burst from the body
so fiercely, to pour
unchannelled from
the five wounds
and the unbandaged brow,
drowning the dark wood,
staining the stones
and the gravel below,
clotting in the air
dark with God's absence.

It was created for
a closed system—
the unbroken
rhythms of human blood
binding the body
of God, circulating
hot, brilliant,
saline, without
interruption
between heart, lungs
and all cells.

But because he
was once emptied
I am each day refilled;
my spirit-arteries
pulse with the vital red
of love; poured out,
it is his life
that now pumps through
my own heart's core.
He bled, and died, and I
have been transfused.

The unveiling

It was God's breath, blowing across
the earth's face, that first polished
the hills with wind, fired them in
the kiln of sun, exposed their
glistening flanks through scarves
of rain. Sky pointers, daily
they balanced glory on their peaks
and plateaus.
                    Often, afterwards,
Yahweh touched the mountain tops with
meaning: unfurling his iridescence
over Ararat and the emptied ark,
igniting a bush with holiness on Sinai,
etching there, on two stones, his eternal
standards (destined for breaking),
flaming in Moses' eyes as he squinted
against Light, planting balm
even on the battle-bloodied sides
of Gilead. Yes, and on Carmel, the Lord
kindled Elijah's soaked sacrifice to fire
and then reversed himself, his hand
like a cloud opening, pouring on
the febrile, fainting prophet the torrents
that ended more than one drought.
                                 Yahweh
did his best business on the heights:
protecting with his zeal the ark of
covenant from Uzziah's brashness
on Moriah, blessing Obed-Edom there
for the same ark's seclusion in his
threshing yard, then raising on that very rock
his own House—hewn stone and cypress
wood lit with gold, traced with angels,
palms, pomegranates—for beauty and
for glory—the terror of his Presence
curtained with brilliant linen. It was on
Moriah that a son had once been saved

from slaughter as the Lord's young ram,
seen white through its tissue of
thickets, rescued Isaac for his father's
faith.

Time and the Spirit lift for us
the last veil, join in one the holy
double image, focus our seeing on
slain Son/sacrificial Lamb (displayed now
as a whole world's ransom) on the one
out-thrusting rind of rock—Moriah,
Zion, Golgotha, Skull Hill—showplace
for God at work.

*"On Mount Zion will the Lord remove the veil that is
spread over all nations."* Isaiah 25:7

*"When they came to the place called the Skull, there they
crucified him . . . and the curtain of the temple was torn
in two."* Luke 23:33, 45

*"Whenever anyone turns to the Lord, the veil is taken
away."* 2 Corinthians 3:16

The sign of the starfish:
Old Lyme, Connecticut
for Paula D'Arcy

With a clutch of debris from the sea
in my hand, wetly translucent quartzes
the shapes of babies' ears,
weather-worn buttons of wood—
I was treading the narrow band
of the beach between waves and sand
when I picked up a starfish. The spell
of the sea and the sky caught suddenly,
and I wondered how we can say for sure
that some galaxy of sea stars isn't shining
up from an uncharted ocean floor,
or that gulls never fly
the submarine blue as if it were air,
or that fish are not darting somewhere
through the Milky Way
past layers of barnacles lining
the rocks at the outer limits of sky,
or that clusters of oysters
and pearls and sand-dollars
aren't lying, tide-stranded
waiting for light-years to be found
as if Someone had handed
his secret sea-treasures around
on some of the shoals of heaven
as well as here, for me, today,
on a shore in Long Island Sound?

The sounding: Snakeshead Lake

Sun skins the morning lake—
a dream, a dazzle I cannot
pierce. It profiles the dark
movers on the surface—the striders,
snakesheads, water spiders—
the beetles, leaves, loons,
with all their clicks, calls—
the beavers, the strict spears
of the reeds.

The water sleeps, waiting
for me to find my balance on
the floating log. I turn, then,
sun at my back, and probe
the milky shape of my own shadow,
sending my senses diving,
sounding the deep home of
the gilled, gilded, finned,
flaming blue-green, evercool,
underworld water-breathers.

How they hang speechless
in their own element, like bees
in amber. They are caught,
like me, in the wet gap
between bank and bank, air
and earth, linking last winter
and the next, targets
of the sun's swords, the arrows
of the eyes, as Snakeshead Lake
and I, multi-levelled,
wait for a new fathoming.

With Jacob

inexorably I cry
as I wrestle
for the blessing,
thirsty, straining
for the joining
till my desert throat
runs dry.
I must risk
the shrunken sinew
and the laming of
his naming
till I find
my final quenching
in the hollow
of the thigh.

Disciple
Luke 9: 57-58

Foxes lope home at dusk, each
to his sure burrow. Every bird
flies the twilight
to her down-lined nest.
Yet come with me to learn
a stern new comfort: the earth's
bed, me on guard at your side,
and, like pilgrim Jacob,
a stone for a pillow.

eucharist

grain cracked
ground   baked
fingered to fragments

      grapes crushed
      casked   splashed
      along tongue

         both tasted
         throat-taken
         gut-gained

blest body
of bread   beaten
to new seed

      joyous juice
      spilled by
      swift spear

         find now fresh
         furrow   harrow
         my fallow heart

At the Church of the Saviour, Washington, D.C.
Summer, 1983

Leaving outside all heat, and the confusion
of self-consciousness, as my own heart's latch
lifts, I enter the door to God's house. The inside
air, cool, blossoms with the scent of multiple
flower heads, and the color.

I find a seat in the circles of others.
As our glances meet, Christ looks out from
the brown eyes and the blue. His presence presses
lightly on us all, each, the unseen hand
moving in blessing from head to head.

Against the wall candles cluster—a benediction of
brown, cream, cinnamon, white—their flames
in the breath-currents moving toward each other
like tongues of fire, like fingers.
In a back row a child makes a soft sound.

A cross unites the space, its arms embracing our
diversity, its shaft both pointing up and reaching
down. As the Word comes incarnate, spoken, broken
once again, love rises in silent incense, in a unison
of silver sound, from four-score hearts and throats.

With Lindsay: watching sunrise over Stewart Mountain

In my heart I see her climbing down from the loft in her
blue robe, clumsy with sleep. Together we stand in
the cold doorway for first light to embrace us, and in my
pocket her small fingers fold themselves into mine.

Time has set it firm and clear in me, not with a
shutter click, but gently as pectin suspends lemon
slivers: the sun mouthing the lip of the peak,
the spikes of pines dissolving in the glare, the dozing
valley shadowed under its sheet of mist. Dawn's
landscape is finished with two invisible roosters, their
antiphons cleaving the vapor between barn and hen-house.

Today the whole meadow is soaked with gold, the fowls
are silent. Lindsay's glance dances back to me along
the seasons. Though under the passages of sun the child
has grown, the barn has weathered, the shingled roof
shows a new crop of stag-moss, all the drifting, lifting
fogs of the Northwest have left no imprint on this
crystal air. The rising sun runs faster than my calculation,
but I know that each lengthening blade of grass, each
weed head is flamed singularly, like a child waking to light.

Three-year-old

Lauren, toe stubbed,
limps sobbing up the stairs,
clings to my knee

Hugging, I lift her to my hip,
my shoulder, till she's high in my hands
as the fork of a tree

Pain gone like a bad past, she begins
to beat a song on my head with her fingers—
"Zaccheus was a wee

little man . . ." she sings, and each
winged note falls in its golden spin
like a sycamore key

Home movie

As we drive East the landscape
develops like a film: seamless prairies
give way to a narrative of forests
spliced with plots of hops and potatoes.
The horizon exposes itself in a suspense
of green crests. Incidental rivers
and other bodies of water unroll
into one—vast, salt, smelling of fish.

Two weeks later, the trip home from the
shore runs the whole vacation backwards:
lobster pots vanish, sand falls from
our shoes, a lost beach towel reappears
like a special effect, the scenery
relaxes into flatness. What if our lives
could be unreeled? Our journey taken over?

Landfall
for Ann & John Gordon

It was evening when we first caught sight
of the low, silent sea-coast—our ship
still pitching in swells rough
with memories of the storm, though by then

the air had died to a breath and a sigh,
and the sky was glowing, cloud-innocent,
smooth as the inside of a shell.
What a time it took us, though—what

alternations of tides and what careful
study of charts all through the night
before we could find the narrow break
in the reef. Finally, at dawn, we let

the rise of the incoming tide lift
us through. Beaches glinted in and out
of the salt fog. Whales, curious, blew
as they sighted us. Gulls urged us on

in their imperious way. The cross-
currents, the barnacled black rocks,
levelled a thousand threats at us
between the crests of the breakers,

before the inlet, visible from only one
angle, revealed itself. Sliding behind
a finger of sand that thickened into hand,
arm, elbow, shoulder, we dropped anchor

at last in the bosom of the cove. There
in that calm enclave, we splashed through
shallows to shore to drink deep of spring
water, the relief of arrival, the bliss

of dry sand under our sodden feet. Later,

circled by the land's embrace, we bedded down
on fixed earth and watched, without fear,
the star voyagers circling their own dark ocean.

Nowadays, along that same shore,
beach houses cluster, and a town behind them.
But some early mornings, when the fog
moves in and lays her wedding veil

along the sand, smoothing the sea flat
with its pale film, we can imagine that place
pure, unexplored, virgin, and begin
to discover it all over again.

Milton Keynes UK
Ingram Content Group UK Ltd.
UKHW040651070124
435594UK00001B/4